10
AMAZING
MUSLIMS
TOUCHED BY
GOD

I DEDICATE THIS BOOK TO my Muslim brothers and sisters around the world seeking to know the way, the truth, and the life of God.

CONTENTS

INTRODUCTION

THE STORIES YOU ARE ABOUT to read in this book are often very special Muslims, some Sunni and some Shiite, to whom God chose to reveal Himself in extraordinary supernatural ways. These men and women represent a vast demographic of Muslims, from jihadists to peaceable leaders, humble Bedouins to intellectuals of various echelons of society, from around the world. Most of them are devout, while others are scholars of the Qur'an and *Hadith*, and some are just ordinary Muslims in search of answers from God. All committed followers of Allah and Islam with a deep affinity for truth in their hearts. Each of their stories and perspectives about Islam are transparent and unique.

In the summer of 2004 while in prayer, a tangible reality of God's presence filled my room and I immediately became conscious of the glory of Almighty God. An angel of the Lord came into the room and spoke in an audible voice to me saying, "I have come from the Throne of the Most High God, The Great God Jehovah and He has a message for you." When he spoke these words, the glory of the Lord went into my spirit and I was overwhelmed by the weightiness of the glory and in awe of the majesty of God.

Then the angel said it again: "I have come from the Throne of the Most High God—The Great God Jehovah and He has a message for you," and once again the glory of the Lord went into the core of my being. Then he left and I remained in the residue of God's Presence and continued to pray, pondering the message of God, over the next three days. When the glory of God went into my spirit, the message was imparted to me; and as I prayed I was able to understand and interpret the message.

Through this message, God unveiled His plan and purpose for the Muslim people and how this plan would correlate with the Jews and Christians in the end times. Along with the message, God also released an impartation of His heart for the Muslim people and an awareness of His love and mercy for all of humankind. This message is contained in its entirety in my book *The Destiny of Islam in the Endtimes.*

Today there are reports of millions of Muslims throughout the world, including the Middle East and Asia, who have had similar experiences to the ten amazing Muslims in this book. Most of them God has spoken to; some He has taken to Heaven to show them the majesty of what Heaven is really like. Others He has rescued in their times of dire need, often healing their bodies and their souls. When He comes to these people, in whatever their circumstances, their lives are changed forever. Being in the presence of Almighty God will do that to you.

The similarities in their stories confirm how God is light and love, along with many other attributes including omnipotent, omniscient, and most holy. At the same time, the uniqueness of their encounters unveil how God understands our deepest needs and is merciful to humankind.

I consider it an honor to journey with you through this book, and I believe as you read you will find answers to some of the deepest questions of your heart. You will be inspired and challenged and at times even shocked. You will hear truths from the Qur'an, the Torah, the *Zabur* (the Book of Psalms), and the *Injil* (the Gospel), along with the ancient prophets of God from the Bible.

Assalamu Alaikum (Peace be unto you),

Faisal Malick

CHAPTER 1

MY QUEST FOR SPIRITUAL TRUTH
Akef Tayem

I AM A PALESTINIAN ARAB, born in Haifa, Israel. My father was a wealthy merchant who inherited and carried on the family business of growing and exporting produce to Great Britain. He was a respected leader in the community, a good father, and a devout Muslim who strictly observed the tenets of Islam. I do not remember much of the home where I lived as a young Palestinian boy, but I do remember my family talking about a big white house in the midst of huge old olive trees overlooking the Mediterranean Sea.

After the partitioning of Palestine, Haifa became part of the newly created state of Israel. Being a proud Muslim, Dad refused to live in Israel. So I was the last child in the family to be born in Haifa. My dad arranged for us all to get on a fishing boat, and we set out to our new destination—the island of Cyprus. The family grew to a total of five boys and five girls when three more siblings were born in Cyprus. We found favor in the eyes of the locals. We soon learned to speak their languages, Greek and Turkish. Cyprus is predominantly Catholic, so it was natural for us to attend the Catholic elementary school, which I entered at the age of six, along with my brother who was two years older than me, and, later, my younger sister.

Being a proud Muslim, Dad refused to live in Israel.

Education was very important to my family. My oldest brother, Muhammad, taught himself English and then enrolled in an American correspondence school. He eventually won a scholarship to Ohio Wesleyan University, in the United States, and later earned a master's degree in mathematics from the University of Arizona. Remarkably, he secured a job as professor of mathematics at Ohio Northern University. Another of my brothers received a scholarship from Wilmington College in Ohio. After graduating, he earned his master's from the University of Dayton in Ohio. He held the high jump record at the English school for about 15 years after his graduation. He, too, taught mathematics, at a junior college in Columbus, Ohio. He later married, had three children, and entered the real estate market, and is now a wealthy entrepreneur. My youngest sister mastered nine languages and found employment with the United Nations.

THE TUMOR

Meanwhile, back in Cyprus in my senior year in high school, a lump began to appear on my right thigh and kept growing. In the beginning, it gave me no pain whatsoever, and I used to make it move by poking it with my finger. At first, we thought nothing of it—perhaps it was a sports injury that would soon go away. However, it did not go away. It continued to increase to the size of a baseball and began to hurt, especially when I walked. It was finally diagnosed as a malignant tumor.

The doctor recommended immediate amputation of my leg to prevent the cancer from spreading to my vital organs and causing my death. A second opinion by a specialist convinced my dad to sign papers authorizing the amputation. I was then moved to the intensive care unit and scheduled to undergo the amputation a few days later—a day or two before Christmas. Then, unexpectedly, the day before the operation my mother checked me out of the hospital, ignoring the doctor's warning that I would be dead in a few weeks.

> I was moved to the intensive care unit and scheduled to undergo the amputation a few days later.

I still remember the little Turkish coffee cup that Mom used to draw olive oil out of a large vase. In fact, it was the largest vase I have seen in my life. When I was seven or eight years old, it was as high as I was tall. I later learned it held over 50 gallons of oil. We had two such vases; one held only olive oil, and the other held olives aged in olive oil, garlic, and herbs.

After checking me out of the hospital, it was from this large vase my mom massaged a cup of oil into the tumor of my bedridden body several times a day. Mom never cried in front me, but I would often hear her sobbing and notice the redness in her eyes when she would come into my room. Yet she would give me hope and promised me that I would not die and that I would grow up and have children of my own some day. Within a few days, she noticed that the tumor had begun shrinking. After two weeks of massaging this olive oil, the tumor had shrunk enough to allow me to bend my leg, and shortly after, it went away completely! The faith of a loving mother is contagious.

Six months after my recovery with a second chance at life, I bid my family and my adopted homeland farewell, and left under scholarship for college in the United States. My priority, like the rest of my family, was education. I planned to complete my studies, get my Bachelor of Arts degree, and then attend law school at Ohio Northern University in Ada, Ohio. I was going to be an attorney.

During my sophomore year, I met a girl of whom I became quite fond. She spoke much about her Christian faith. I made it clear to her that I was a Muslim and I was not interested in any other religion. There were no mosques nearby in my city, but that did not matter because like all Muslims, my entire life was patterned after my faith in Islam. My college years were during the "hippie" generation. My belief kept me from doing drugs and other things that were going on at that time. My roommate in college was a cocaine addict. He tried many times to get me to "just try it one time." I never did. I went to clubs with friends but never had any alcoholic beverages, and I never smoked "grass." The fact is that I was not even tempted to do so. I knew my religion forbade it and that was good enough for me.

I SAW A MIRACLE

The girl I was dating became unbearable when a "faith healer" set up his tent close to the college campus, babbling on and on about miracles and healings. I was convinced he could be nothing more than a char-latan preying on naïve people. Nevertheless, I liked the girl, so I went to the tent meeting with her. The flamboyant man, who looked to me more like an Elvis Presley impersonator than a minister, had taken a young child with a deformed leg and placed him on the stage declaring that Jesus was going to heal him. He called out for any agnostics and skeptics present, especially students (since this was a college town), to come on the stage to get a closer look. I did not hesitate and went up for a closer look.

The child was a young boy no more than six or seven years old. His right leg was in some sort of leather brace, but his leg was clearly vis-ible through this contraption. It was much thinner and shorter than the healthy one. The preacher sat him on a chair and removed the brace. He extended both of the child's legs, supporting them with his left hand. I could see that the withered leg was three to four inches shorter than the normal one. The preacher picked up a microphone with his right hand, and he began to pray, asking Jesus to heal the little boy. The au-dience, as if on cue, suddenly rose from their seats and extended their hands toward the stage. In an instant that startled me, the withered leg extended itself to the same length of the other leg! Just as suddenly as it grew, it stopped growing. Then, as if someone blew air into it, like blowing air into a balloon, the leg "puffed up" and looked just like the healthy one! Apparently, the incident also startled the child. It took him a few moments to get his bearings and stand on both legs. He took a few clumsy steps and then seemed to gain confidence with each step. Soon after, he was running full throttle around the tent as the audience cheered him on.

> *Deeply impacted by this miracle I witnessed with my own eyes, I was down on my knees sobbing and weeping uncontrollably.*

It was spectacular! Awesome, to say the least. I am not exactly sure what happened to me next or how it happened. Deeply impacted by this miracle I witnessed with my own eyes, I was down on my knees sobbing and weeping uncontrollably. My consciousness was arrested by thoughts of Jesus and my heart was searching for answers. I didn't believe in miracles, and Muhammad the prophet of Islam never performed miracles. My Muslim mind could not process what had just taken place. I had no idea what a profound impact this would have on my life and where it would lead me.

MY FAMILY DISOWNS ME

I did not tell my family about the experience. But to myself I kept thinking that if Jesus had healed that boy's leg, that had to mean that Jesus is alive! The only person I confided in was my brother who attended the Catholic school with me when we were kids. He just tried to talk me out of it. He told me he was sure it would all go away as if nothing ever happened. He told me to stop talking about Jesus and this miracle. I tried speaking to him a couple more times, but his response was the same: Renounce and forget about Jesus and continue to walk in the path of Islam. At that time I considered myself a Muslim, but I still could not renounce the possibility of the reality of Jesus; it was not even within my power to do so. Jesus never left my thoughts after the tent experience. Not even for a second. Some might think this is an exaggeration, but it wasn't. I had seen too much. The only explanation was that Jesus had healed that boy!

When my family was finally told what had happened at the tent meeting, they tried to persuade me to pretend it never happened. But I simply could not do so. Ultimately, and because of my profound reaction to this experience, my family disowned me. My dad explained to me why he had to do what he did. I told him I understood.

> *The only explanation was that Jesus had healed that boy!*

Shortly after this, my friends, my family, and everyone I had known all my life seemed to conveniently disappear. Somehow my life did not matter anymore. I needed to try and sort things out and sought comfort in solitude. I felt restless and just wanted to get away, but I had nowhere to go. Only one place came to mind—a small town in the suburbs of Birmingham, Alabama. I had briefly met an older couple at the tent meeting. They told me how pretty the South was—the terrain, the trees—and that they lived close to the vicinity of a spectacular view the locals call "God's Country" in Gadsden, Alabama. They had given me their address and asked me to come visit them should I ever be in the vicinity.

> *My friends, my family, and everyone I had known all my life seemed to conveniently disappear.*

With nowhere else to go, I started heading toward their house in Alabama, while still undecided as to whether I should go or not. I just kept driving, too restless to stay put. After a couple days of driving, and about 1,000 miles later, I found myself driving through very dense forest that was scarcely populated on my way toward their home. I drove for almost 30 minutes in this forest. The scenery was breathtaking—especially when compared to the two-dimensional terrain back in Ohio. The only thing that reminded me that people must have been living close by was a little, white, wood frame country church on a deserted dirt road in the woods, right in the middle of nowhere. I had no intention of stopping, but something made me—perhaps the serenity, perhaps the solitude, or both. But now I know, due to what followed, it had to have been God leading me.

MY QUEST FOR TRUTH

It was around noon on a Sunday when I pulled up to this very small country church. It couldn't have seated more than 50 people, though there were less than a dozen cars in the church's rough parking lot and only about two dozen people in attendance. The minister was a woman of some age who introduced herself as Sister Prince.

> *It had to have been God leading me.*

I started to explain who I was and what I was doing there. I wanted to tell her what happened at the tent. I wanted to say, "I am a Muslim—a Muslim thinking about Jesus all the time!" Perhaps she could explain it all to me.

She opted to remain silent. Perhaps she knew what I needed was silence and that I had a void only God could fill. As I tried to explain myself, she kindly interrupted to tell me that I was welcome to stay for as long as I wanted, and that I did not need to explain anything to her. "You are in God's hands and He will take good care of you," she said with a smile and an assurance I so desperately needed. I immediately felt at home.

This place was so incredibly quiet and serene that I felt at ease for the first time in a long while. I decided that if I could stay there for a few days alone, I could sort things out. Then I would head on to visit the couple or just get back in my van and return to school. Perhaps the trip was all I needed to help understand exactly what happened that afternoon under the big white tent when the boy got healed. And so there I stayed. There was no housing, so I slept on a pew. There was not even drinking water in the building, only a shallow well at the back behind the building with water unfit for drinking. I was told about a shallow stream in the woods with clean, cold, and drinkable water that flowed year round.

> *"You are in God's hands and He will take good care of you," she said with a smile and an assurance I so desperately needed.*

While searching for the water, I found what became my favorite spot deep in the woods, marked by a large sandy white rock. I would go every day. It was summertime in Alabama—hot and a little humid—but I loved the solitude. I passed the time reading a Bible someone had handed me at the tent. It was the only tangible thing I had from what happened in the tent. I had many questions and was aware of the Bible being the Christians' holy book, just as the Qur'an was the holy book for Muslims. I had this unexplainable, burning desire to read it, so I started to read.

ALONE WITH GOD

After a while, as if in a time warp, I suddenly realized I had been there about a week and had not eaten anything the whole time. It was not because I did not have money or transportation to go eat. Besides, the church people left me several covered dishes daily on the last pew next to the door, especially on Wednesdays and Sundays, though I did not see anyone during the days I was there. I wanted to be alone, and I guess they left me alone physically but not in their thoughts because they brought me the food and someone left two gallons of water for me on Wednesdays and Sundays. I was not fasting and in no need of dieting. I simply had no appetite. I realized that a lack of nutrients would take its toll on me, but I did not worry because I knew I could leave at any time. However, it just did not happen that way. Days turned into weeks. I lost track of time and did not know how long I had been there. I later calculated it at between five and six weeks—just about 40 days.

> *I was not fasting and in no need of dieting. I simply had no appetite.*

Near the end of this time, I had become quite weak and could barely make the journey back to the church. I tried to make one more attempt to reach the church from my place near the stream. As I was coming up the hill, the view of the church and the empty parking lot came in clear view. My van was no longer there! I panicked as the incident shocked me back to my senses. I was now ready and determined to leave this place as soon as possible. I decided to turn back and go to the stream as I was hoping the water would rejuvenate me enough to make it to the dirt road by the church where I hoped a passing motorist would see me.

A VISION OF MY HEART

As I walked back in the direction of the stream, I had a vision that still amazes me to this very day. In the vision I saw a human heart that was alive and beating. Inside and moving about were what looked like small tentacles. They were hideous and disgusting—a ghoulish sight that would captivate any Hollywood horror movie director. I was in total disbelief and angry with God, myself, and everyone else when I realized I was looking at my own heart. How could this be? I thought I had been living a relatively clean life. I did not drink alcoholic beverages, do drugs, or smoke. I was honest and never set out deliberately to hurt anyone. It simply made no sense. The burden was simply too heavy for me, and despite my reading of the Bible, I felt God was nowhere to be found!

I found myself on my knees weeping and in desperation as I begged God not to distance Himself from me. He was all I had left. Then the most difficult experience of all happened. As I recall, it only lasted a very short time—perhaps seconds, perhaps minutes. In an instant I realized that all my "good works" gave me absolutely no credit in Heaven. In that one moment I felt I was totally immersed in darkness and I felt a complete separation from God. It was the worst, the hardest moment ever in my life. I experienced a void that was without the existence of God, like how it would be if there was no God. At that moment I felt like I would rather live for a moment with the knowledge of God than an eternity without Him!

I did not understand it at first because I thought I was "acceptable" to God because of my good deeds as a Muslim. At the tent I had seen a mighty, powerful Jesus who can do miracles. Now I began to understand why Jesus died on the Cross for my sins! It was this moment that made me realize the relevance of Jesus in my life and how I need Him in order to enter Paradise.

> *It was this moment that made me realize the relevance of Jesus in my life and how I need Him in order to enter Paradise.*

I abandoned my search for the stream of running water because I could barely walk and I felt so faint. I picked up my Bible. It was my habit to read loudly so I could hear the words echo in the woods around me. The sound of my voice also helped break the monotony of the silence. As I opened my mouth to pronounce words, I realized I was extremely dehydrated. I felt pain in my lips as my action had torn the skin. I felt blood streaming down my chin. The skin between my fingers was cracked and tore like a piece of dry and aged paper. I could barely walk. I prayed for rain—it was my only hope—but there was not a single cloud in the sky. I started getting dizzy. Things around me seemed out of focus. The trees seemed to be upside down. They looked as if they were hanging from the sky. I started to pass out, but then I quickly felt myself slip out of my body.

MY OUT-OF-BODY EXPERIENCE

The next thing I remember was being about ten feet above my rock looking down at a person whom I did not recognize. He was very thin—all skin and bones—with sunken eyes and parched skin that looked dry and bruised. He lay there by the rock beside an open Bible. It was me. The only phrase I could see clearly in large red letters said, "Fear not, only believe."

I started moving upward, surrounded in darkness, toward the sky. I was not aware of how fast I was moving or of any other details. The only thing I could think of was that I had no weight. I had a form, but it was without substance. I could put my hand right through my own self if I wanted to. Soon after, I found myself passing through a well-lit area and then back into darkness. This went on two more times. When I came to the third well-lit area, I stopped. I stood on what appeared to be wool. I realized that the reason I could stand on it was that I had no substance, and that if I had any weight, I would fall through.

> *In front of me, about ten feet away, I saw the form of a man taking shape. I knew in a split second that it was Jesus.*

In front of me, about ten feet away, I saw the form of a man taking shape. I knew in a split second that it was Jesus. I do not know how I knew, only that I knew it was Jesus. It was more like a silhouette of Him. I could not make out any features, such as the color of His eyes or hair, but I could make out the outline of a robe and what seemed to be shoulder-length hair. He began walking toward me, stopping when He was within arm's length and He said, "Touch Me." The sound of His words came from everywhere—above me, beneath me, behind me— from every direction. I reached out my right hand and touched Him just below the rib cage. I stopped when I realized that the tips of my fingers actually went inside His chest.

The next thing I knew, I was back on my rock. I was alive—and it was pouring rain! When I woke back up at the rock after hearing the voice of Jesus and touching Him, I was a new man. With the healing of the boy's leg months before, I had seen the power of God, but now I had touched the Lamb of God! I danced my way back to the church, completely restored to life. No words can ever describe my experience with Jesus.

The ride I was hoping for earlier came along and I was picked up by Cecil Cornelius who was a deacon of a local Baptist church and also the local barber. I told him what had happened. He took me straight to his pastor. They insisted that I go to the hospital for a checkup. I begged them to give me a couple of days and if, by then, they still wanted me to go, I would. Cecil and his wife let me stay in their home. I took a long bath. They gave me soup and crackers to eat—my stomach could not hold solid food. The mere smell of food cooking made me want to vomit. They said I slept all day and all night. When I woke up I felt like a new man. They told me I looked like it too!

After recovering my strength, I went back to the little white church where I had stayed for several weeks and visited and told them what happened. I was also asked to share my testimony by the pastor and his wife at the church where Cecil was a deacon. As I was relating the event, I noticed that my right hand, the one with which I had touched Jesus, was red, sweaty, and felt very hot. I was bewildered and perhaps even a little scared. The audience noticed my concern and so did the pastor, who interrupted me to ask me if I was all right. I showed him my hand. He held both of my hands and commented about how much warmer the right hand was. A few in the audience began coming toward the stage, and before I knew it, many people from the congregation who wanted to feel my hand had come up and surrounded me.

> *As I was relating the event, I noticed that my right hand, the one with which I had touched Jesus, was red, sweaty, and felt very hot.*

MIRACLES FROM MY OWN HANDS

Now this church didn't believe in miracles any more than I did as a Muslim. But one of the people who came forward to see my hand was a gentleman who was a deacon and who had been in a wheelchair for 30 years. He reached out toward me and I touched him. Inside me I just wanted him to get out of that wheelchair—and he did! He got out of the chair and took a step, then another, and soon he was walking all over the church. He even went outside walking!

The word spread. From then on, whenever I would share my story of coming to know Jesus, many amazing things and healings would take place. At an Assembly of God church where I was invited to hold a three-day meeting, an old lady approached me at the end of one of the meetings. She told me that because I have a heavy accent she could not understand much of what I said, but she said, "Something about you keeps bringing me back. God is all over you, son."

> *Years before, Jesus had healed my own leg from the tumor, though I did not know He did it at the time.*

Jesus healing the leg of a boy had captured my heart. Years before, Jesus had healed my own leg from the tumor, though I did not know He did it at the time. It was entirely supernatural. Only He could have. All my life He had been protecting me, leading me on a path to Himself. Islamic law dictates that Muslims who walk away from Islam should be put to death. What many people do not know is that leaving Islam for Jesus does not bring a "punishment as an apostate" but rather the redemption of one's soul. I put my life on the line for my faith in Jesus. My reward is His presence with me at all times.

CHAPTER 2
JIHAD TO FREEDOM
Kamal Saleem

I HAD A DREAM AS a child. I was dressed in the long white shorts Muslim children wear and was riding a white horse. In each arm I held a double-edged sword. In front of me stood the enemies of Allah. They were Jews and Christians. I cried out, "For Islam!" and ran into the battlefield. Their elite warriors came at me and I challenged them, causing chaos among them. I conquered them and took off their heads with the sword so that their heads were rolling under the feet of Allah. In my dream I was martyred, and when I came before the throne of Allah, he was laughing and said, "Only my crazy Kamal could do this."

This was my Islamic worldview from childhood. The dream reflected the Sunni beliefs of my family. *Jihad* for me was birthed from infancy. Our home was Lebanon. To me it was beautiful and heavenly. My father was my hero as a child. I looked forward to seeing him when he came home, usually with two leather bags with food. I could smell the metal on his body as he was a blacksmith. He understood steel and he understood hard work. My mother came from an Ottoman Turkish background and believed with all her heart that the ultimate Ottoman Empire will rise again to rule and reign.

> *My mother taught us what it meant to be a Muslim, and how Muslims had conquered the world and would do it again.*

Our home was a three-room house where I lived with my 13 brothers and sisters. It was like a bunker at night—one side for the boys and the other for girls. It was tragic, but only 11 of us lived past our childhood. If my mother or sisters did something wrong, my dad would do something harsh to them. In Islam, the men are often in charge of the women and the women answer to the men, so that's how it was in my family.

MY PARENTS TAUGHT ME TO HATE

My favorite place was the kitchen. It was where I learned things about Islam from my mother. She taught us what it meant to be a Muslim, and how Muslims had conquered the world and would do it again. She taught us the Qur'an and the *Hadith* (writings of the eyewitness accounts of the deeds and sayings of Muhammad the prophet of Islam). She was a very passionate teacher. Even other women came to listen to her teach. My siblings and I were taught to recite the Qur'an with our mom as she chanted. She made sure we understood that whatever we do in our lives, small or great, we would reap after death. My father would explain it this way, "Allah will weigh all your deeds both good and bad and whatever tips the scale, means Heaven or hell for you." I knew as young child that my life must be about working my way to Heaven. In Islam our works and deeds are the only chance to enter Heaven other than martyrdom.

Around that kitchen table I learned from my mother that the Day of Muslims would not come about unless we fight, according to the *Hadith*, the book of the deeds and sayings of Muhammad, the prophet of Islam. I understood from my mother about the conquering Islamic war. She said, "If you kill a Jew, your hand will light up before Allah and the host of heaven will celebrate your killing." We kids practiced killing on the cats and dogs in the neighborhood.

> *We kids practiced killing on the cats and dogs in the neighborhood.*

I learned what my fate would be. Not only must I work for my future, I must meditate each night on how to conquer the world and how to bring Islam to the world. I loved Islam and Allah and Muhammad and all he said in the *Hadith* with all my heart. I learned from childhood that I was going to change the world. I was willing to die for Islam—even my mom said so.

I believed all along, just as the 9/11 attackers did years later, that I could do bad things and then, if necessary, I could die as a martyr and still have a one-way ticket to Heaven. My father taught about martyrdom. Every Muslim will have to pass through hell first (see Qur'an: Surah 19:71). When a martyr dies, the first thing that happens is he becomes an intercessor, and because of his martyr's death, his family can go to Heaven without being judged. So families rejoice when a son becomes a martyr. A martyr also receives 72 virgins at his death. I said to my dad, "You only have mom and you have issues with her. How are you going to have seventy-two? How am *I* going to do this?" He said the grace of Allah would be sufficient.

We interpreted the Qur'an as Muslim zealots. Moderates were seen as infidels who must be Islamicized. I learned as a child not to be afraid to lie about things. We were taught that it is OK to lie—not against a Muslim, but against any enemy of Islam. If we were asked to spy on the enemy, we were to lie about them. Whatever one says for the sake of Allah and for Islam is forgiven. (This is a doctrine called *Al-Taqiyah*.) I was taught that one of the 99 names of Allah is "the Greatest Deceiver." In the *Hadith*, Muhammad said specifically that if a Muslim ever takes an oath and finds it's more beneficial later to do something against the oath, he can then do the better thing. Muslims can do *anything* for the sake of Islam. Small sins or big sins, it doesn't matter.

At the age of five, I was going to the mosque and fasting at Ramadan, with my mother's help. I was learning in the mosque how to conquer the infidels. We were to conquer the world, specifically the United States and Israel. America is considered the throne of satan, where he resides, while Israel is the second satan. We were taught that they must be destroyed. America is the final frontier. If we conquered America, we could conquer the whole world. These were the principles I was learning as a child.

> *Muslims can do anything for the sake of Islam. Small sins or big sins, it doesn't matter.*

When I was seven years old, my father took me out of school to bring in finances. I was forced to work for my uncle who lived on the other side of town. I worked all week for three dollars. My uncle would beat me if I was late. If he could not get out of me what he wanted, he would slap my face. I had to walk there, which required that I walk through three areas—the Armenian Christian, Kurdish, and Shiite neighborhoods. I woke up late one day at 5:30 A.M. On the way I was beat up by some mean teenagers. They stole my shoes, umbrella, and my lunch. My cheek was cut and I could not see out of one eye. I was bleeding everywhere. I took refuge in a mosque. The Imams saved my life that day. From that day on, my life was different.

These Imams were holy men. What they taught me as a child shaped my life. *Islam* means "submission." The translation in Arabic means you are not just a servant but one who seeks to please. The teaching of this submission to Allah is that we have the right to take over the whole world as Muslims. We have to usher in war in order to bring Islam to the world. We have to fight for the land of Israel and go to America because their women, their children, and even their economy legally belong to us.

> *We have to fight for the land of Israel and go to America because their women, their children, and even their economy legally belong to us.*

THE MUSLIM BROTHERHOOD

One day a man came to our mosque and talked to us about the Muslim Brotherhood. The Muslim Brotherhood is made up of people trying to spread Islam through war. He said, "You have the power of the Qur'an; now you can have the power of the sword." The Muslim Brotherhood is one of the most radical organizations in the world. Al-Qaeda finds it roots in this organization, and many other radical groups do as well. This recruiter was a representative of the early Palestinian Liberation Organization (PLO), which was called Fatah at that time. Our whole group joined. I was the youngest.

I went to my first PLO assault camp at the age of seven. The first day I went to the camp I was completely taken with it. I saw the biggest playground I ever saw. Dangling ropes over mud holes to jump over. Flat walls to jump and climb over. I had no toys, and now these were the biggest toys imaginable. But they weren't for playing. We were to approach these things as warriors. These men lived war. They smelled like warriors and looked like warriors with their long hair. This was not a class trip; we were here to learn war. My life took a turn that day.

One of the leaders looked at me. He said, "Child, do you want to be a warrior?"

I said, "I am a warrior!" as I slapped my hand on my chest.

He said, "You cannot be unless you know how to use a weapon." He took up an AK-47. He choked it and handed it to me. The smell of the steel reminded me of my father's shop—bold and strong. I was familiar with that smell. It entered me. He taught me how to hold it. I learned how to go from one shot to automatic. "Now shoot," he said. I shot 30 bullets into the heavens that day with an AK-47 and fell in love with a rifle. I knew at that moment I was transformed. I loved the feel of the steel in my hands. The gun became my friend, and the smell of gunpowder became my addiction. It robbed me of my soul.

Now I had the word (Islam and the Qur'an) and the sword (the AK-47). I wanted to be that warrior for Allah and live like these men and one day fulfill my childhood dream.

> *The gun became my friend, and the smell of gunpowder became my addiction. It robbed me of my soul.*

Not only could I now handle a machine gun, but I learned how to make bombs and how to slip into enemy territory to use the gun and the bombs. We trained on and on for weeks. Besides knowing how to shoot howitzers and automatic weapons and use TNT blocks, we were taught how to slit throats, how to pierce a man's liver and kill him in five seconds, and how to drown someone underwater.

> *The breaking of our spirits came at a young age when our moms and dads taught us this was the path.*

One day we were practicing going under barbed wire, in preparation for going into Israel, while a 50-caliber gun was shooting over us with live ammunition. One of my friends peeked over the barbed wire just to see. His head is still there! He was killed instantly. I didn't realize until that moment how real this all was.

A JIHAD WARRIOR AT SEVEN YEARS OLD

What happens to the mind of children who are exposed to that dehumanization? The breaking of our spirits came at a young age when our moms and dads taught us this was the path. The Imams taught us hate and anger with the intent to take over the world for Islam. Then they would send us into killing fields to desensitize us to murder. We were programmed to believe that this was how we were to live our lives. We were completely broken, like a horse that now accepts the rider and obeys the bit in his mouth, or like a dog that was trained so he knows all the tricks.

Now, at seven years old, I was a liberator, determined to liberate everyone to whom I was sent. I was sure I would change the world. I started recruiting other children who wanted to be like me.

MY FIRST MISSION

My first mission at that young age was to smuggle duffel bags with TNT blocks and AK-47 ammo into the Golan Heights in Israel through Syria via underground tunnels. (These tunnels are like the ones dug between Gaza and Israel or the ones dug from Mexico to the U.S.) We would rendezvous with some shepherds at our drop point and then they carried the ammunition and explosives to the *Fedayeen* (Arab commandos) to kill Jews. My first mission was a success and when we got back to our base, hundreds of men and women celebrated us by shouting *victory* and *Allah is Great*. Now I really thought I was going to change the world!

I was given my next mission to the Golan Heights, but this time I was to lead the group of young warriors. As we grew closer to our drop point something did not feel like the first mission. The yoke seemed heavier and I was so scared. I wondered if Allah was watching me. I told myself I could not be weak—I must set an example for younger ones.

As we approached the other side we heard a swarm of flies. We kept moving forward toward the rendezvous point and there was no sign of the shepherds and all the sheep were lying down. Then we saw the color scarlet and realized that blood was everywhere. We were about to abort the mission when suddenly a rocket fell and bullets started coming at us from the Israelis. Everything slowed down for me as if time was stopping. I was crying out, "Mama!" I heard other kids crying for their mothers too. One of them got shot. My eyes were searching for my friend Mohammed. When I spotted him running toward me, shrapnel cut through his body. Something ushered me up on my feet. I grabbed my friend Mohammed and threw him over my shoulder and started running to the Syrian border in hopes of preserving myself from the Israeli fire. In all the chaos I couldn't find where the tunnel was. As I ran toward where the Syrian army was, the rockets stopped, but the Israeli bullets continued, like snipers from behind me.

> *My friend had become my shield. I started screaming, "I promised your mother I'd bring you home alive!" But instead Mohammed died that day.*

I heard something like little rocks hitting Mohammed. I crossed over the border and laid him on the ground. My friend had become my shield. I started screaming, "I promised your mother I'd bring you home alive!" But instead Mohammed died that day. I came to know what death is in a different way.

MY ENCOUNTER WITH YASSER ARAFAT

A special guest I will never forget came to visit us in the PLO camp. It was my proudest day! I got called to a mandatory meeting. I went and was ushered up to the special guest. He was Yasser Arafat. They put me right on stage with him. He was wearing his *keffiyeh*, a traditional Arab headdress, a symbol of Palestinian nationality. I felt like I was seeing the prophet Muhammad. He started speaking and hailing the movement. "Children like you," he said and pointed at me and other kids, "will change the future. You *are* the future."

He stepped forward and continued to say, "People like Kamal will liberate Jerusalem for us one day." Then he grabbed me and I almost had a heart attack. I was being touched by the great Arafat! He grabbed my head and kissed me on my forehead and put me next to him as he spoke. "Go with me," he said as he put a white scarf and a red beret on me.

> *I traveled the world on one mission after another— whether it was to surprise Jews and kill them on the streets or to kill Russians in Afghanistan.*

That was just the beginning. From that time on I traveled the world on one mission after another—whether it was to surprise Jews and kill them on the streets or to kill Russians in Afghanistan.

In Saudi one of my favorite things was to watch the beheadings on Friday afternoons of the infidels—those who wanted to leave Islam for another religion or those who were gay or lesbian. I had tasted blood and I'd seen death. I was on one bloody mission after another. This was my resume. In my heart I was lifting up the banner of Islam and changing things in the world for Allah. I felt powerful because I had been chosen. I admired men like Muammar Gaddafi and Saddam Hussein. I thought to myself, *Maybe I can be that man who will change the world. I can conquer Jerusalem. I can open her for my people. Jerusalem is our land, after all.*

Libya belonged to Muammar Gaddafi, Iraq belonged to Saddam Hussein, Syria belonged to Hafez al-Assad and they were all trying to conquer Jerusalem. *Maybe I can be the one to do it.*

> *Not all Muslims want to kill. The radicals, however, believe that the moderate Muslims must be killed or become like them.*

There are two kinds of Muslims. Of the 1.5 billion total Muslims, 18 percent are Islamists who want to kill. Not all Muslims want to kill. The radicals, however, believe that the moderate Muslims must be killed or become like them and live by the Qur'an and the *Hadith*, which is a record of everything that Muhammad did and taught. The radicals have a code that they live to liberate the world from the Jews. We were taught that the Qur'an says that no one will be left except the Muslims. The Jews and the Christians will be no more. We were taught that God so hated the Jews that He caused them to be monkeys. Cleansing the earth from Jewish blood was the goal. As for the land of Israel, it's Muslims against the Jews. We write on walls in the Mideast: "The people of Saturday (those who hold the Sabbath on Saturday) first and the Sunday people next." First we will annihilate the Jews, then the Christians. This was the mindset I had as a radical Muslim Jihadist.

In classes we were taught both the philosophical and military aspects of Islam. One class was the propaganda class. How do you turn everything against your enemy? In Lebanon we shot our weapons from hospitals, from United Nations locations, and from schools, so that when the Israelis hit back at where the rockets came from, innocent people died. We were even using children and women as shields. It was a tactic so we could spread propaganda about the Jews killing innocent people, women and children. This way we could say, "Look who the Jews are killing!"

The political party Hamas would do this, too, to garnish sympathy from the world for the Palestinians and create propaganda against the Jews.

AGENT FOR CULTURAL JIHAD

My heart's greatest desire was to see the giant infidel dead. That great giant is America. I came to the United States for the purpose of cultural jihad, determined it would change America the way it was changing Great Britain and Europe. I worked with the Muslim Student Association, the Young Muslim Association, and the Muslim Brotherhood. There are many groups with the goal of cultural jihad in the United States, and we were working to unify them.

> *My heart's greatest desire was to see the giant infidel dead. That great giant is America.*

Our first target was the ethnic groups like the African Americans and Hispanics in the prison system. We would tell them, "The white system put you behind bars and forgot about you. Islam came to free the black people from American slavery. We are here to give you freedom."

Another tactic was to knock on the doors of lower income families and the poor people. We would ask them, "What do you need today?" or "Are you hungry?" Then we would buy groceries and cook for them. Over time we would befriend them and ask them to join our cause. We would tell them there's no God but Allah and Muhammad is his final prophet and messenger. Once we earned their trust we would then begin to indoctrinate them with the ideologies of Islam. Then we would meet their families and help them find jobs and meet their needs and so on.

Unlike 9/11, cultural jihad is about becoming like the enemy in order to conquer the enemy from within. You have to learn the language and the culture; you have to learn to eat, speak, and blend into society. Another focus for me was to take Christians and Jews and convert them to Islam. These in return would become Muslims who would bring others to Islam and help pave the way for America to be vulnerable to Islam from within and without.

> *Cultural jihad is about becoming like the enemy in order to conquer the enemy from within.*

I got a job and proceeded to be a "nice guy." I would help meet people's needs, be a friend to them, all to win their trust in me so I could then bring them to Islam. I used to go to high schools, to colleges, and to the prison system. I would tell people in the prisons, "Allah wants to take care of you." When you go to people who are outcasts of society and you tell them Allah sent you to help them, you don't have to sell it. They're ready for help and for Islam.

In order to conquer the world we were also taught to work in the Western world specifically through the women. Women would be easier to convert to Islam.

"The America women are easy," we were told. "Tell them you love them and before you know it they will fall for you." The strategy was to marry them and acquire a green card and citizenship. The next step was to spread Islam to her family and friends. Now we could change the culture from within the family, with a goal to subdue the world and bring it into "submission" to Allah.

A CHANGE OF DIRECTION

One day something happened that changed my life completely, just when I thought everything was moving in the right direction. I was driving down a street when a truck came from the opposite lane and hit me head on. The impact was so severe that I ejected out of my seat and out of the car. Parts of the car landed on my neck, so that I could not move my body. I was severely injured. I was taken to a hospital. As I lay in the hospital I had only confusion. *Why had this happened?* I thought maybe Allah was angry with me.

> *The family took me in as if I were part of their own family. Their children treated me with love, something I had never known before.*

Two doctors and another man became very close to me during my time in the hospital—the orthopedic surgeon, the physical therapy doctor, and a "Good Samaritan." Since I had no family in America, one of the doctors and his wife befriended me and took me to their home to recuperate. I stayed there the entire time it took me to recover. The family took me in as if I were part of their own family. Their children treated me with love, something I had never known before. At seven years old in my life I had been a jihad warrior. But now, these kids were speaking to me without any violence in their thoughts. They were touching me, loving me, and praying Jesus prayers in their little voices for me to recover and be healed.

I WANTED A RELATIONSHIP WITH ALLAH

This kind of relationship with their God was so new to me. Allah was not a god of relationship as far as I knew. All of a sudden I wanted a relationship with him. But in Islam you don't have a relationship with Allah. He's up there and you're down here. You are a servant and he is a distant god. But I decided I would seek Allah and see what he had to say.

One day I fell on my knees in front of a window and put my hands up to Heaven and cried out to him, "Allah, Allah, my lord and my king, why did you allow all this to happen to me? Allah, why did you put me among these people? I'm confused. They are stupid. They don't know who we are or what our capability is. Allah, why did you do this to me? Allah, I'll kill more people for you; I'll make more Muslims for you. I'll change the world for you. I want to have a relationship with you. If you are real, speak to me. Let me know that you are real."

I waited.

Guess what Allah said? Absolutely nothing.

While I waited, this family flashed before me and became like a living book in front of me. I started to see how they lived their lives. They had a relationship with their God and with one another as husband and wife. They were Americans *and* Christians, but they were not bad people as I had always believed. They took care of me, revived me, loved me unconditionally, and prayed for me. They were generous and tender to their children and they lived by a different code called love that I didn't know existed. I certainly didn't know how to love. We sought to "love" our enemies by causing them to vanish through terrorism. These people lived by their Bible that says to love your enemy and to take care of the people who are homeless or in need. I was both—homeless without any family to care for me and greatly in need. They were reaching out to me. What's more, they paid my hospital debts! Their children just loved me and called me "Uncle Kamal." These people even trusted me to baby-sit the children.

> They had no idea that their deadly enemy was in their midst.

They had no idea that their deadly enemy was in their midst. I thought, *I could finish the whole family off in one moment. They are like sheep to the slaughter.* Yet I also realized, *But they are not what I have been taught.*

I thought, *I can't live anymore because everything I lived and worked for is not real. It's false. And when I needed Allah the most, he did not come to me.*

At this point I was desperate for answers and worried Allah might kill me for questioning him. Islam teaches that if you challenge Allah he will kill you, and I had challenged him. I thought, *Allah, if I die today because I kill myself and I go to hell, I will be glad to go to hell because I called you and asked you and knocked on your door and you did not do anything.* I was sure the sword of Allah would come right then and take off my head.

THE GOD OF ABRAHAM CAME TO ME

I wanted to clock out that day, to put an end to my life. I thought, *This is the final place for me.* I was reaching for one of my guns that I still had with me to blow my head off. At that moment, suddenly, for the first time in my life I had a miracle. I heard a voice that had to be God's. It was so real. The voice was kind, gentle, and meek, like a father's voice, like He knew me as a child, even before I was born. He called me by my name and said, "Kamal, the Muslims believe in the God of Father Abraham; the Jews and the Christians believe in the God of Father Abraham. They all pray to him. Why don't you call on the God of Father Abraham, Isaac, and Jacob?"

If the voice hadn't mentioned Muslims, I would have thought it was a demon speaking to me. I fell on my knees with my hands reaching up to Heaven and very swiftly cried with all my might, "God of Father Abraham, Isaac, and Jacob, if You are real, will You speak to me? God of Father Abraham, if You are real, I want to know You!"

That's all I had to pray. The God of Abraham came to me. The God of Heaven and earth came right there into the room. The room was filled with His tangible glory and power. In His Presence was fullness of joy, power, healing, love, peace, assurance, and reverence. It was Jesus and He just stood there, and I said, "Who are You, my Lord?"

He said, "I AM that I AM."

I said, "What is that supposed to mean?"

He answered, "I am the Alpha and Omega, the Beginning and the End. And I am everything in between. I knew you before I formed the foundation of the earth. I have loved you before I formed you in your mother's womb. Now *koome* (rise up) Kamal. You are My warrior; you are not their warrior."

As I rose up, my body was impacted from top to bottom. My head, my neck, my collarbone, my ribs, my knees—everything became perfect. He totally healed me in one moment. Only the God of the Bible did miracles. He did not do miracles in any other religion. Surely not in Islam. At that moment I knew His name was Yahweh, and His name was Jesus, and I understood that God is one. I said to Him, "I will live and die for You, my Lord."

But He said, "Do not die for Me. I died for you that you may live."

> The creation came to know the Creator for the first time in his life that day, and the creation surrendered.

I said to Him, "I will go and grab them by the eyelashes and the skin of their teeth and make them Christians!"

His response was, "The harvest is plentiful. The workers are few. Be an ambassador of Mine."

I started jumping up and down and shouting, "I am the ambassador of God!"—only to realize later there are millions of ambassadors.

The creation (me) came to know the Creator for the first time in his life that day, and the creation surrendered. Someone I didn't even know made me. I knew who my mother and father were, but it is God who created me! It is He who has marked my life and the life of every believer in Jesus.

I have a different mission today—to love my enemy. Today my heart's desire is changed. I no longer desire to hate my enemies or kill them. Now I give His life to those I thought were my enemies and the people I desired to kill, the Jews and the Christians. Today I stand on their wall guarding and watching over them!

The Bible says that he whom the Son sets free is free indeed! (See John 8:36.) My journey from jihad to freedom and liberty took place in Christ. If I did not meet Christ I would never ever have had a story of victory to tell. One god (Allah) sought my blood; the true God gave His blood for me. Islam called me to be his slave, and God called me to be His son. One arrested my life; one set me free. One blinded my eyes; one opened my eyes. If I have anything to say to my fellow readers, it is that today can be a beginning for you. Won't you call on Jesus today, the God of Abraham, Isaac, and Jacob, the Great I AM?

COMMENTARY BY FAISAL MALICK

It may be hard for you to imagine how a jihadist Muslim warrior since the age of seven who traveled the world killing Jews and Christians can be a recipient of such mercy and love by calling upon the God of Abraham, Isaac, and Jacob.

Abraham was the father of Muslims, Jews, and Christians long before Islam even came into the scope of humanity. Muslim people find their roots in Ishmael, who is an ancestor of Mohammad the prophet of Islam. Father Abraham and his son Ishmael have always been important to Muslims.

Growing up as a Muslim, I remember celebrating the "Festival of Sacrifice" (*Eid al-Adha*). Each year at this festival my family would sacrifice an animal, as Muslims around the world still do today. My dad would purchase the animal and we would get to feed it and take care of it in preparation for the festival. The purpose of the festival was to sacrifice an animal to honor and remember how God provided a ram (male lamb) for Abraham to sacrifice in place of his own son. Muslims believe this son to be Ishmael. The Torah, which is part of the Bible, however, records this son to be Isaac rather than Ishmael.

When Abraham was on the way to the mountain designated for the sacrifice to offer his son, the Bible records that Isaac inquired of his father, the prophet and friend of God, where the lamb was for the sacrifice. Abraham confidently responded and said:

> …*God will provide Himself a lamb* (Genesis 22:8 KJV).

What an amazing prophetic declaration: "God will provide Himself a Lamb!"

Our own father Abraham long before the Qur'an even existed looked into eternity and saw a glimpse of the Lamb of God, slain before the foundation of the world, who would one day come to earth and take away the sin of all humankind (see Rev. 13:8; John 1:29). Abraham, as a prophet, was speaking of Jesus who was yet to come and die on the Cross as God's own sacrificial Lamb.

Before Abraham's knife could touch his son, an angel of the Lord called out to Abraham and stopped him and showed him a ram that was caught in the trees. This male lamb was a symbol of Jesus the Lamb of God who would one day come and die on the Cross.

When Jesus walked the earth He even acknowledged that Abraham saw him, shocking the religious leaders of His time by saying:

> *Your father Abraham rejoiced to see My day, and he saw it*
> *and was glad* (John 8:56).

In response to the religious leader's question as to how Jesus could have met Abraham from generations before He was born, Jesus simply explained, *"...before Abraham was, I AM"* referring to Himself as God, and using the same words, "I AM" that God spoke to Moses at the burning bush, which of course the Jews were very familiar with (see John 8:58; Exod. 3:14).

> *Jesus referred to Himself as God, and it is for this reason specifically that the religious leaders of his day wanted Him crucified.*

Jesus referred to Himself as God, and it is for this reason specifically that the religious leaders of His day wanted Him crucified. But God had foreordained that He would die this way.

This is what Kamal was trying to understand when Jesus said, "I AM that I AM" to him. This is how God revealed Himself to Moses. This is why when Kamal called out to the God of Abraham he encountered Jesus, who is the Alpha and the Omega, the Beginning and the End (see Rev. 21:6).

To further clarify this mystery of Jesus, the Word of God coming to earth as a sacrifice for all of humankind, let's look at this important biblical reference:

> *And without controversy great is the mystery of godliness:*
> *God was manifested in the flesh, justified in the Spirit,*
> *seen by angels, preached among the Gentiles, believed on in*
> *the world, received up in glory* (1 Timothy 3:16).

The Word of God was manifest in a human body and this Word is Jesus. This is why the Bible says that God was manifest in the flesh. This is also the reason why Jesus (the Word) was born of a virgin. He is the Word that became flesh and walked among humankind. Both the Qur'an and the Bible acknowledge that Jesus is the Word of God and was born of a virgin.

Abraham saw Jesus, Moses saw Him, and even Kamal saw Him and his life was changed.

CHAPTER 3
LIVING A SUPERNATURAL LIFE
Faisal Malick

AS A FAITHFUL MUSLIM BORN in Pakistan, I believed that Allah sent many prophets, the final one being Muhammad whom Muslims follow and to whom God gave the Qur'an, which is the only book from God that we believed to be unchanged. I was committed to studying it and loved reciting it. The Qur'an was my primary purpose of life. In our Muslim culture, our entire lives proceed from our faith. For a Muslim, faith is not a part of your life, it *is* your life! And so we were willing to die for our book, for the Qur'an. All this I came to know and believe without question as I was raised to believe.

My parents visited Niagara Falls on the American-Canadian border while on a three-month world tour on their honeymoon, and my mom fell in love with the place. Eventually they moved to Canada, which was when I was still a young child. However, when I was seven years old my father died, and my mother moved us back to Pakistan in order to keep me from being absorbed into the North American culture. She wanted to be sure I grew up with a strong Muslim heritage.

Back in Pakistan I continued to be raised in a devout Sunni Muslim lifestyle. After school I would go to learn the Qur'an for three to four hours every day. There I was taught to recite the Qur'an and be a better Muslim submitted to Allah, the highest name of the 99 names of the one and only true God and creator of Heaven and earth. My mom eventually remarried a devout Muslim man, an accomplished attorney, who became my stepfather. I observed his faith and gleaned from him as well. My grandfather on my mother's side was also quite a spiritually astute man and I gleaned from him as well.

As a young man I did well in school and also took an interest in working. From the age of 14 I started to teach and provide private lessons to students for a tuition fee. I had quite the busy life but was always willing to take on responsibility around the house.

> *I thought the Christians exalted a man and made him to be equal with God.*

At the age of 17, I left Pakistan and moved back to North America. I lived on my own and went to school in order to become a successful businessman and make my family proud. While in the process of my education, I got involved in business and came in contact with some Christians whom I believed were deceived because they lacked the truth of Islam. I respected Jesus, but as no more than a prophet and one who was second to Muhammad, the final prophet of Islam. I thought the Christians exalted a man and made him to be equal with God. Therefore I considered the worship of Jesus blasphemy. I also believed, as I was taught, that the Bible was corrupted and changed by Christians. I believed the greatest sin a Muslim could ever commit was to confess that Jesus is the Son of God.

My passion, though, was to help these deceived Christians, and if possible the Jews, to ultimately accept the Qur'an as the final book of Allah and become Muslims. As a result, many discussions about faith began— although actually they were more like arguments than discussions. Around that time I got involved in a network marketing business. A Christian associate invited me to church, and I remember saying to him, "I am a Muslim. I do not need to come to your church." He never seemed to argue with me and let it go.

When a big network marketing convention took place, I attended, desiring to learn more about business from people who were already successful in life. Among the 20,000 people there I met many Christians. Soon I was debating with them, trying to change their incorrect thinking.

GOD AT A BUSINESS CONVENTION

At one of the conventions an announcement was made that they were having a non-denominational (Protestant) service on Sunday morning in between sessions. I was told that if I came to the service, I would be given a front row seat and I could keep the same seat for the rest of the business meeting. This was an opportunity to get a good front row seat. And since the man speaking wasn't a pastor or priest but one of the business people, I took them up on their harmless offer. When I walked in, the whole front area was empty, about the size of where 30 or 40 rows of chairs could have been. I suggested to someone they put in more chairs. But the answer was, "No sir, something will happen here," referring to the empty area.

> *Muslims don't have an assurance of Heaven, but there is assurance of hell if you even think Jesus is the Son of God.*

Then the speaker arrived and he began to speak. Of all the things this businessman could have said, what he did say made me really angry. He started out by saying Jesus is the Son of God. There was no more blasphemous thing he could have said than that a son of God even exists. If I confessed this, it would send me straight to hell. Muslims don't have an assurance of Heaven, but there is assurance of hell if you even think Jesus is the Son of God. How could God have a son? The Qur'an forbids such blasphemy to even consider such a thought. I wanted to confront and debate this speaker.

The man continued to quote from the Bible saying that Jesus is the way, the truth, and the life and that no one comes to the Father except through Jesus. This was so entirely different a perspective from what

Muslims believe. This was a reversal of what I have always believed—that Allah is not a father and he doesn't have a son—but this man was saying the total opposite of what I had always believed. He went on to say that Jesus paid the penalty of humanity's sins and if you don't accept Him but reject Him you will burn in hell forever. I did not like this statement either. He also said that if you receive Jesus that you will be guaranteed eternal life with God in Heaven. I was surprised he was sure about how to get to Heaven because as Muslims there is no assurance of salvation.

Then the man said that the Bible is the only true Word of God and the other one is not. I was even more angry because I knew he was now referring to the Qur'an. My thought was that this man was entirely deceived and I needed to correct him. Then he began to give an invitation for people to come to the front to respond to his message. I suddenly realized this was my opportunity to confront the man, and so I got out of my chair and ran to the front area thinking I could confront him. But before I could speak to him, others came from all over the coliseum running to the front to respond to his invitation. My first thought was that they were coming after me to ambush me. I didn't know what was going on! I thought I had better get out of there. I tried to leave, but I couldn't get through the crowd. I was stuck where I was, right at the front of the stage.

I looked up at the speaker and he had tears in his eyes. He asked everyone to repeat a prayer that started out with affirming that Jesus is the Son of God. While the others prayed with him I just repeated the *Kalma,* my own statement of faith, saying, "Allah is the only true God and Muhammad is his final messenger." They may have been praying what they believed was a prayer of salvation, but I was saying what I believed. At the end of the service, as I was leaving, a few friends came and hugged me and congratulated me. They thought I went forward to become a Christian. "I am not a Christian," I told them emphatically. "The earth can shake, the mountains can move. But nothing on this earth can make me confess that Jesus is the Son of God!"

> *"I am not a Christian," I told them emphatically. "The earth can shake, the mountains can move. But nothing on this earth can make me confess that Jesus is the Son of God!"*

After the convention I continued to work to convince Jews and Christians about Islam. But as I wanted to learn how to be a better businessman, I went to another business conference to learn more. Again I was on the front row. Again I went to the altar to try to talk to the man. That's when I realized they were using their business platform to win people to Christ. I made a decision I would learn from them so I could win people to Islam by sharing the Qur'an and giving invitations like they were doing. I was already in business, but I intended to use my life to bring these Christians, in particular, to come to Islam. I only knew enough about the Bible to know the supposed flaws in the Bible, but I thought it was enough to prove them wrong. I started to pursue my goal with more intensity, and over time I did get familiar with what Christians believed so I could counteract their beliefs with the Qur'an. However, it was only a short while until God interrupted my agenda.

"THESE ARE MY CHILDREN."

I attended a third conference to learn more, but now I knew not to respond when the man called for people to come forward. Once again, I was on the front row. This time the man said, "If you believe in Jesus He will give you the right and power to be sons of God just by calling upon His name." Shortly after his message the man asked everyone to stand and all 20,000 people did. Now that I knew I didn't need to respond I thought I didn't need to stand, but out of courtesy I did so.

> *The moment I stood, suddenly God Almighty manifested in Majesty right in front of me.*

The moment I stood, suddenly God Almighty manifested in Majesty right in front of me. Instantaneously, I was standing before Almighty God and every fiber of my being became aware of Him and His mighty Presence. His Presence went through me and circled me—I was alone with God and I was experiencing the majesty of God. The Living God came upon me! Suddenly someone stood before me. He was taller than I am, over six feet tall. His Presence went right through me. Many thoughts were going through my mind. I had one burning question that I managed to ask Him: "God, what are *You* doing *here?* I thought these are the bad guys." I couldn't understand why He would come where people were blaspheming God by worshiping Jesus.

He answered me audibly and I heard His voice say to me three times, "No, these are My children. No, these are My children. No, these are My children."

> *I knew with every fiber of my being that Jesus is the Son of God.*

I had thought these people were the deceived, but He was saying these people were His children. As a Muslim I didn't question that there was one God. And I knew I was encountering God. But I surely didn't believe God was a Father. Yet at that instant I *knew* He was the Father. I knew with every fiber of my being that Jesus is the Son of God. I suddenly knew who Jesus is! It was revelation to me. In fact it was the only reality I knew at that moment. At that moment, Jesus was revealing the Father to me so I instantly understood that God Almighty was not only Father, but I was encountering God as *my* Father! I didn't know this could happen. I certainly didn't try to make it happen. But when I heard His voice, it vibrated through my entire being. When God speaks He releases a sound, and everything responds to it. The very core of my created being was awakened to Him.

I FOUND THE TRUTH WHERE I LEAST EXPECTED IT

The very thing I had been trained to see as deception and that was so ingrained in me to disbelieve was the very revelation that I now knew: Jesus is the Son of God. The very statement I said I would never say was the revelation I had now received: Jesus is the Son of God. His voice shattered every belief system I ever held. And with the sound of His voice, I came to see there is no other truth but Jesus. That day I stepped forward into that empty area and confessed that Jesus is the Son of God and He came to earth, was born of a virgin, died on the Cross, shed His blood, and rose again from the dead. I asked Him to come into my heart so I can love the Father even as He does. This happened to me on Sunday, July 3, 1994.

What was the most difficult thing for a Muslim to accept or understand about Jesus became the foundation of my revelation of Him—revelation that came directly from God. After I accepted Jesus as Messiah, I had to process some of my Muslim ideas and schools of thought. How could Jesus be the Son of God? Jesus was not just an ordinary Man, but He existed from before the foundation of the earth and is the Word of God that came from Heaven to earth as Man. (I will shed more light on this in my commentary after I finish sharing more of the journey with you.) I had a revelation like Peter did in the Bible where he knew that Jesus is the Son of God. It was the Father who revealed it to him. Only the Father can reveal the Son and no one can reveal the Father except the Son. The Father had revealed His Son to me! My mind did not understand it all yet, but I knew it was so in my heart. Revelation that comes from the Father overrides what our minds have been taught and opens our hearts to faith in the truth.

MY CONVERSATIONS WITH GOD

Allowing revelation to change my thinking was an important step in walking out my new faith. When I first met Jesus I became aware of

God the instant I had the encounter. I knew I could talk to Jesus and just as suddenly, God became a Father to me. At first I was a little nervous and shy with Him. I knew He was listening to me. *Ishmael* means "God hears" so I was aware that God heard my prayers. But when I would speak to Jesus, He would gently lead me to the Father who would love me and talk to me and whisper to me, "Do you know why you are My son? Do you know you are a unique person, and do you know now you have purpose? Why? It's because of My Son Jesus." So my love for the Father was also for Jesus.

My encounter led me into a journey where God began to teach me. Jesus led me to get to know the Father, and the Father taught me to know the Son. When I met God, I met Jesus; when I experienced Jesus, I experienced God. Jesus is the Word of God who pre-existed before the foundation of the world.

HOW I WENT TO CHURCH

I had run into some people in a Greek restaurant parking lot whom I heard talking about baptism. I went that Sunday night to their church. As I sat in the crowd, I sensed the Holy Spirit telling me to get baptized. I told the pastor I needed to get baptized. He told me to come back and to do it another time. I said, "No, I need to be baptized tonight." After speaking with me he agreed, and I was baptized that night. I started to go to church regularly from then on.

LIVING IN THE CAR

I was now living in Canada and caring for a rental property for my parents. My family abroad had heard rumors from the Muslim community that I had been hanging around with Christians, and they were suspicious that Christian influence would corrupt me. So they gave the power of attorney to sell the house I was living in to their friend. One cold winter day I came home and the locks had been changed. So I started to live in my car. I did not want to be a trouble to anyone, and financially I was out of options too. I parked my car at a hotel parking lot at night to camouflage myself while I slept in the car overnight. I would sleep sitting up and turn on the heat intermittently.

> *My Muslim, Hindu, and Sikh friends attributed my circumstances to being the result of having turned my back on the God of Islam.*

I remember my Muslim, Hindu, and Sikh friends attributed my circumstances to being the result of having turned my back on the God of Islam. I knew differently and responded to them with the only revelation I had, saying, "Whether I live in a car or a mansion, I know Jesus is the Son of God." I was not mad at them, but instead I had this overwhelming peace and consciousness of God's presence. The revelation of the Father and His love was greater than my circumstances. I also knew He would take care of me, and He did. Later I moved out of my car into a small room that would be best described as a basement of a basement.

MORE GOD ENCOUNTERS

On Friday, February 24, 1995, at 7:30 A.M., the Spirit of God came and His holy Presence filled the little room I was now living in. I was surprised as I thought He only came to large crowds, like at the conference I had attended. It was as if someone took the entire Pacific Ocean and fit it into a bottle. Suddenly this holy Presence of God like a deep mighty river began flowing through my being from the top of my head through to the bottom of my feet. It was pure love and the substance of Heaven, the very life of God. The Bible says a river flows from the throne of God and the Lamb (Jesus) from above (see Rev. 22:1). This experience continued tangibly for three hours.

In the midst of this river I also heard an audible voice speak to me, words I never heard in all my life growing up as a Muslim. It was the voice of the Father, and He said, "I love you, son! I love you, son! I love you, son!"

I could do nothing else but respond to Him saying, "I love You, Father. I love You, Father. I love You, Father."

I got up off the floor at 10:30 A.M. and noticed three things that had changed about me. First, I had an intense love for God like I never had before and an intense hunger to know Him more. Second, I had a much deeper, unconditional love for people. Third, I had an intense love and supernatural hunger for the Word of God. I picked up the Bible and could not put it down for 36 hours straight. As I looked at each page it would explode inside my heart and my understanding was opened. The Holy Spirit became my Teacher and was writing His Word on my heart. I supernaturally read the entire Bible in 36 hours and could not eat anything. This verse became reality to me: "...*Man shall not live by bread alone, but by every word that proceeds from the mouth of God*" (Matt. 4:4; see also Deut. 8:3-4).

> I picked up the Bible and could not put it down for 36 hours straight.

FRUIT THAT FOLLOWED

From that moment on, a special grace was upon me, and this river of God and began to overflow into others. I changed that day, and the fruit was evidenced in the fact that 99 percent of the people I knew—including Jews, Hindus, Sikhs, Muslims, and atheists—gave their lives to Jesus and were born again. It was truly by the Holy Spirit and by me yielding to the river of reconciliation, the Spirit of God, that approximately 1,500 people came to know Christ. The Word was now in my heart and it became alive to me. I supernaturally understood the Bible. When I spoke the Word to others or prayed for them, the substance I had experienced in the river of God overflowed into their lives. God interrupted our conversations with His presence and people would begin to weep. The tangible presence and an awareness of God was so real that when I met people, they experienced something too. They said things like, "You really know this God. I want to know this God like you do."

> *The tangible presence and an awareness of God was so real that when I met people they experienced something too.*

I often met people at a Perkins Restaurant that was open 24 hours. I usually brought one of these recent converts with me so they could learn from what God was doing. Let me share one interesting Perkins story. A Muslim man had been coming out Sunday nights to Perkins where I was gathering with some of these new believers. He would come around, but he never surrendered his heart to Jesus. One day after a lunch meeting I shared some more truth with him about Jesus. He left and went home offended, but to my surprise he returned again for coffee that Sunday night. He spoke with another Muslim for a little while who had just become a Christian too, and then he came to speak to me and said, "I am ready to give my life to Jesus." I inquired as to what made him ready and his answer was this: "Every time over the last two years that I've come around you, this presence comes on me, and when I go home it leaves. Today after our lunch meeting this holy presence that I know is God followed me home and will not leave me. I know I must surrender my life to God."

Well, we prayed together and this Muslim man became a follower of Jesus and his life changed. He was experiencing the presence of Almighty God in the person of the Holy Spirit. I pray you may know and experience the Holy Presence of God as well.

GOING BACK TO PAKISTAN

The time came to go back to Pakistan and tell my family. I had not seen them in six years and I wanted to go to honor them. Three times prior God had kept me from going to see them, but this time I knew I would share my faith with them. A relative in the U.S. had sent them word to tear up my Canadian passport and not allow me to leave the country of Pakistan because this person knew I was involved with Christians and thought I may have become corrupted.

When I arrived at the airport in Pakistan, my stepfather saw me first. He is a reputable criminal attorney, a man with a high level of perception. He saw me and determined that I was not what they were saying about me. He told the family, "Our son is a holy man of God," just by looking at my face. He thought it was all rumors. Later, when I was in the house with my family, they made this statement, "We smell the stench of Christianity on you." They then followed up that statement with a demand that I say the *Kalma*, the Muslim confession of faith. I responded, "I'm sorry. I cannot do that." Their response was even more awkward, "Then what do you have to say?" I answered, "Jesus is the Son of God, born of a virgin. He died on the Cross, then rose from the dead, and now He lives inside of me."

That shocked them and they didn't know what to say. So I got my Bible, which was under the bed. I had hidden it to read it secretly. They were further shocked that I had a Bible. I shared the truth with them about Jesus. They were quite moved and did not know what to say.

WITCHCRAFT IS NO MATCH FOR THE POWER OF GOD

Shortly after this incident, God revealed to me that witchcraft was being done against me. Witchcraft and sorcery is very common in Pakistan. I told my mother and the rest of the family there was someone conducting sorcery against me. My family was shocked again that I would know this. It was not long before the son of a woman who was a witchdoctor came over to the house and provided confirmation, saying his mother went to meet with a well-known warlock in the city. This served as natural evidence that what I had known supernaturally was indeed true.

> When the weightiness of God's glory came upon me, I couldn't move. I could see through the walls, however, and heard the voices of someone speaking in another realm.

I went into my room and was lying in bed when suddenly the weightiness of God's glory came and settled upon me. Immediately I recognized the weight of God's mighty Presence. I had learned through previous experiences that when God's glory comes, it's best not to do anything. Do nothing! When the weightiness of God's glory came upon me, I couldn't move. I could see through the walls, however, and heard the voices of someone speaking in another realm. The witches had sent the demons after me. But I was in the glory, so I didn't experience any demonic activity because the devil can't enter or touch you in the cloud of the glory of God.

When I came out of the glory experience, the son of the witchdoctor was still there. He asked permission to visit with me. I told him, "If you want to stay with me you have to get permission from your mother." I told the son that if he would drive me there, I would be glad to ask permission for him. So he graciously drove me to her house.

When the witchdoctor saw me come in, she backed up, turned pale, and began to shake. The residue of the glory upon me began to proceed into her house. She kept frantically moving her head and looking in the direction where she suddenly saw evil spirits leaving her premises. I perceived them leaving also, but I think she literally saw them. She knew these demon entities and they weren't staying around. Shocked, she asked me, "What do you do? How do you pray?" She was astonished how this could be happening. I just said, "I know God personally." She asked me to come back for another meeting before I went back to Canada. I knew she intended to have another meeting with a more powerful witchdoctor and have another round of attack on me. I was not threatened because I knew the power of the shed blood of Jesus.

Days later, I recognized again that witchcraft was being done against me. I knew it supernaturally by the Spirit of God. This time my family believed my supernatural insight from God. The glory of God came on me once again, and this time I also perceived that the evil spirits went back and attacked the woman. As soon as I came out of the cocoon of God's glory, I called her son and said, "Come pick me up because I promised to see your mother before I leave." He came and picked me up, but halfway to the house he stopped the car and told me when his mother found out

I was coming she begged him not to bring me to the house and nervously left the house in the event that I might come.

God's Presence is real and His power is real! If you follow Jesus, He will not only cleanse you from sin but also deliver you from any demonic oppression and all the powers of darkness.

> *Whatever demonic entities were assigned against me must have scared the woman and tormented her instead of me.*

Muslims are not supposed to engage in any form of witchcraft, but a lot do because they're hungry for power. Sometimes Muslims in difficulty who see no solution turn to other spiritual remedies. But they have no powers or guarantee over darkness or demons. Sometimes these Muslims turn to sorcery and give themselves over to demonic possession in order to seek revenge for bitter hurts in their own lives. Sometimes in this process they get hurt themselves when they violate their parameters. When these individuals tried to do witchcraft against me, the glory of the Lord came and I was protected. Whatever demonic entities were assigned against me must have scared the woman and tormented her instead of me.

My family was very moved by these experiences and had me pray for them for healing and divine protection against all the witchcraft. However, a few manifestations of power do not guarantee salvation. My family told me, "We love everything that has changed about you except the Jesus part." Even this amount of acceptance is a lot for a Muslim family. Often they try to kill you. I said, "Without Jesus you can't have the rest."

COMMENTARY

As you read my story, I want you understand that I never expected the supernatural things that happened to me, nor did I try to make them happen. Whether you have a supernatural experience or not, it is important for you to consider what I am about to share with you. As a Muslim, the most difficult thing to grasp is a Christian saying Jesus is the Son of God. As Muslims, we think Christians are suggesting that God gave birth to a son through Mary and therefore, as a result, He has a Son. In other words, we assume that Christians believe that *at the moment* of the virgin birth Jesus became the Son of God. *Nothing could be further from the truth!*

I want to clarify something and shed some light on what the Bible actually says and what Christians believe about Jesus. We are going to look at the Holy Scriptures. The Bible is one of four books that the Qur'an commands Muslims to have equal faith in. The words of the Bible proceeded from the very mouth of God and are the result of the Breath of God, preserved beyond scrutiny through the ages.

> **For unto us a child is born, unto us a Son is given:** *and the government shall be upon His shoulder: and His name shall be called Wonderful, Counsellor, the mighty God, the everlasting Father, the Prince of Peace* (Isaiah 9:6 KJV).

"For unto us a child is born, unto us a Son is given...." When Jesus was born of a virgin, a *child* was born. I want to be very clear that the above verse does not say a *Son* was *born*, but it says a Son was *given*. The *Injil* (Gospel) also confirms this by saying that the Father *gave* His only begotten Son. So the first thing to recognize is that Jesus the Son of God pre-existed long before He came to earth to be born of a virgin. Here is more revelation about Him before He came to earth.

> *In whom [Jesus] we have redemption through His blood, even the forgiveness of sins: who is the image of the invisible God, the first born of every creature: for by Him were all things created, that are in Heaven, and that are in earth, visible and invisible, whether they be thrones, or dominions, or principalities, or powers: all things were created by Him, and for Him: and*

He is before all things, and by Him all things consist (Colossians 1:14-17 KJV).

Jesus is before *all* things; there's nothing that He is not before because He is the source, the root, and the seed. He is the very Word that created *all* things we see and do not see, and through Him alone they exist. This aforementioned verse is speaking of Jesus *before* He was born of a virgin. It was the Word Himself who was conceived in Mary's womb. (The Qur'an and the Bible both acknowledge Jesus as the Word of God.)

> *Jesus the Son of God pre-existed long before He came to earth to be born of a virgin.*

Jesus is the Living Word of God. Let look at another text from the *Injil:*

In the beginning was the Word, and the Word was with God, and the Word was God (John 1:1 KJV).

"In the beginning was the Word...." The first part of the verse goes back into eternity when God created all things—the things that we see and we don't see. We know that the Word created all things.

"The Word was with God...." The second part of verse goes further back in eternity before time—before anything was ever created, and even then the Word was with God.

"The Word was God...." The third part of the verse goes even further back to when the Word was in God. This is before the Word came out of God. Now let's look at the next two verses.

*The same was in the beginning with God. All things were made by **Him**; and without **Him** was not any thing made that was made* (John 1:2-3 KJV).

In the second sentence of the above (*Ingil*) text, the Word is referred to as "Him." Now we begin to see that the Word is a person. This person is

Jesus Christ, the Son of God. He is the Word who came out of God, the Word who was with God, and the Word by whom all things were created, both seen and unseen. He is the image of the invisible God. He is the express image of the Father and the brightness of the glory of God (see Heb. 1:3). We are talking about Jesus before He even came to the earth. This person, the Word, came into the world that was made by Him and unto a people to whom He gave light and life—for as many as came to know Him.

> *That was the true Light which gives light to every man coming into the world. He was in the world, and the world was made through Him, and the world did not know Him* (John 1:9-10).

This Word then became flesh and took the embodiment of flesh to walk in the world among humankind. This Word was born of a virgin and became a Man and lived among us.

> *And the Word became flesh and dwelt among us, and we beheld His glory, the glory as of the only begotten of the Father, full of grace and truth* (John 1:14).

This Word then revealed unto us the glory of the invisible God. This Word is a person and His name is Jesus Christ.

The *Injil* also says:

> *No man hath ascended up to Heaven but He that came down from Heaven, even the Son of man which is in Heaven* (John 3:13 KJV).

Jesus says in John 3:31, "*…he that is of the earth is earthly…* [but] *He* [Jesus] *that cometh from Heaven is above all*" (KJV). Jesus is the only one who came from Heaven. That's why John says no one has seen the Father except the Son. No one has seen His shape, no one has seen His form, and no one has known Him except the Son who comes out of the Father and proceeds forth from the Father:

> *Out of His fullness we have all received grace in place of grace already given. For the law was given through Moses; grace and truth came through Jesus Christ. No one has ever seen God, but the one and only Son, who is Himself God and is in closest relationship with the Father, has made Him known* (John 1:16-18 NIV).

The same Jesus, who is the Word, became flesh and was crucified on the Cross. The Word became the Lamb. The Bible gives the account of John's vision describing Jesus:

> *...And He was clothed with a vesture dipped in blood: and His name is called The Word of God* (Revelation 19:13 KJV).

There can be no argument who this person is as mentioned in the above verse. The *Injil* also calls Him the Lamb of God who takes away the sins of the world (see John 1:29). He is the Lamb who died on the Cross and who shed His blood, which would remain forever a sign that He is the Lamb of God. Because He fulfilled the Scriptures in every way, He is the Word of God. He is the Son of God who was given to us. He is Jesus who loves you, gave life to you, and also died for you. Abraham offered his son as a prophetic shadow of when God gave His only begotten Son—for our redemption and salvation.

Let this thought saturate your heart: Jesus is the Word of God who became flesh, who eternally existed in all creation, and who created all things. He was with God, was in God, came out of God, and is God. He came to earth, dwelt among us, and voiced His Father's will. He died on the Cross, rose again from the dead, and returned to the Father. *He is the Alpha and Omega, Beginning and the End.* He loves you and is coming back again so you can be with Him forever!

I will let you digest and think about that. Now let's continue to walk through the rest of the stories together in this book, and when you are ready, just bow before Him and say:

Jesus, You are Lord. You are the Word of God. You are the Son of God and You are the Lamb of God. You are God manifest in the flesh. You died for my sins and You rose again from the dead. I surrender my life to You and desire to know You and know the Father through You.

CHAPTER 4

SOLD TO THE BEDOUINS, BOUGHT BY THE KING
Khalida Wukawitz

WHEN THE SIX DAY WAR broke out in Israel on June 6, 1967, my mother was pregnant with me. She was injured in the war, and a cousin came and moved her from Gaza to Bethlehem, where a few days later she gave birth to me. Eleven days later, she died. No one knew where my father was, so I was put in a Jewish orphanage even though I was of Palestinian descent. I wasn't the only Palestinian child there. There were approximately 36 of us in the home including several adults who cared for us. Our foster "parents" treated us well and raised us like Jews. The orphanage people became my family. We spoke both Hebrew and Arabic in the home. We had a house in Lebanon where we went for the summers and another house in Jericho. When I was nine years old, there was much fighting going on between Israel and Lebanon. But we children were well sheltered from knowing much about the war.

A ROCKET FALLS FROM THE SKY

One day I was sent to go get water from a well. I don't remember which house we were living in at the time, though it may have been summer, but

I do remember that the house had no running water. On my way to the well I heard a horrible sound of a crash or explosion. I felt the impact. I looked back and was stunned to see that the whole orphanage had been destroyed! A rocket or a missile from an airplane had dropped on the house and killed everyone in the house—all the adults, the teenagers, and the babies. No one ever knew if it was from the Lebanese or the Israelis. The house was completely shattered. It sounded and felt to me like the sky fell to the ground. It was terrifying! For a while I couldn't breathe. Everyone around me was screaming. I was surrounded by chaos. All the neighbors and the police came, but no one took me in. I was the only one who walked out alive except for one other little girl a few years younger than me who had gone for water with me. Her name in Arabic means "grace." Some people took her away and I never saw her again.

> *All the neighbors and the police came, but no one took me in.*
> *I was the only one who walked out alive.*

Now I was all alone in the world. An Israeli soldier found me wandering around crying. I had never seen him before. He didn't know me and I didn't know him. He was in a military vehicle and had a few other soldiers with him. They asked me where I lived. I spoke Hebrew to them and they realized I was from the orphanage. Since no one came to claim me, and they saw I was so upset, they put me in the jeep and asked me where I wanted to go. But I didn't know any address to tell them. They didn't know what to do with me.

SOLD TO THE BEDOUINS

They ran into an Arab man and talked to him and told him what was going on with me, and he said he would take me. So they gave me to this guy. He was an older man, maybe in his 50s. I got in the car with this Arab man. We went over the bridge between Israel and Jordan, the King Hussein Bridge near Jericho in the desert area. At some point I fell asleep. All I remember is waking up and seeing that we were on the bridge.

After we crossed the bridge, the Arab man took me to a marketplace where everything under the sun could be found. In that marketplace he met with a man. They were speaking in Arabic and I could understand them. The man was talking about a price of three to five shekels. "She's strong," he was saying. The other man said, "No, she's not. She looks like she's small. That's the wrong price." I didn't know they were talking about me at first, but they were. They never asked me my name or anything. The new man looked rough, like he'd not had a bath for a long time. He had a long beard and was dressed in Bedouin clothes. I knew what Bedouins were from the market at home. He gave the first guy five shekels and said, "I'll take her." Then he said to me, "You belong to me. Now you're my servant." So I had to go with the rough looking guy.

We walked several miles and then we ended up where there were camels and people. I had been sold to the Bedouin people and I became their servant. That day I became part of a caravan of camels, a dog or two, some horses, and plenty of kids. There were lots of people—about 75 of all different ages—who all lived together. The tribe was called the Hassan tribe.

> *"You are a Muslim now."*

My new owner introduced me to his pregnant wife. They already had kids older and younger than me. When he bought me, I wasn't covered in the Muslim way. I had nothing on my head or long clothes. As a nine-year-old I wore shorts most of the time. The wife said, "You need to cover your head. You'll live with us and your job will be to go get water and to gather food. We don't pay you for living with us, but we give you food and shelter and you travel with us." She was dressed in Bedouin clothes. She spoke Arabic; it wasn't the Arabic from the city where we lived, but I could understand them. She gave me a cover for my head and said, "You are a Muslim now." She began to teach me how to pray. "Obey," she told me, "or you will be beaten," and she described to me how they beat the children. Then she told her son Ali, "Take her to get her camel." I was assigned a camel. It was a six-month-old male camel that became my responsibility. They gave me a stick and taught me how to train the camel.

The tribe followed the Muslim practices and I soon loved doing them. They had their own Imam who led their prayers. He taught us the Qur'an and all the rules of Islam such as the five pillars and about jihad. They taught us to hate the Jews and to never trust them, and to never give any information about ourselves to anyone. Though the Jews had only been like a loving family to me, I came to believe what the Bedouins told me.

I was a good girl and a bad girl. When I didn't do things right, they got upset. I did not sleep with their children. There was another girl like me in the caravan. The two of us did what they asked us to do. If we were late when they sent us to do something, we were beaten. We were not treated as family. We weren't allowed to eat with them; we ate the leftovers after they finished eating. But they became my family—I knew of nothing else.

We traveled in caravan from Lebanon to Syria, from Egypt to Saudi, and back again as a nomadic tribe. I traveled with my camel and lived the caravan lifestyle. At times we were in the desert for three months straight. We baked our own bread and we ate cheese, usually dried cheese. When a baby was born they would kill a lamb to celebrate—two lambs for a boy, one lamb for a girl—but only on such occasions. When we were near the cities we could go inside the market and buy flour. We took the camels to load up. Sometimes we stayed put for a month, depending on where the food and the water was. Occasionally it got dangerous, and people drove us out of an area. Sometimes the conflict was with other caravans. The men of the caravans would fight and kill each other. Whoever lost the fight had to go.

Living in the desert, we often had no food or water. During these years I used to have dreams. I didn't understand my dreams, but I had wonderful dreams in the desert. I heard music and pleasant things were in the dreams. They were peaceful. One time I was so hungry that my stomach hurt. I fell asleep in the desert with my camel. In the dream a man came to me with wonderful food. I could not see his face, but he was urging me to eat and feeding me wonderful food at a table. When I woke up, my stomach did not hurt and I felt as if I had just eaten a wonderful and satisfying meal. I was no longer hungry, as if the dream was real. I wondered, *How could a dream be to my body as if I had a meal?*

> *I didn't have any parents. I was only a servant, so I took care of myself.*

I didn't have any parents. I was only a servant, so I took care of myself. At one point we settled in an area close to Gaza, inside Israel, in a desert area, not too far from the city. A half a day on a camel would take us to the city. A fight broke out. This time it wasn't with other Bedouin people but with soldiers. They asked us to leave. The tribe I was with refused. Our men had knives and guns and they were ready to fight, but the soldiers told the men that they didn't have a choice. "Leave," they said. This was not about food and water. This was more. There was much cursing and fighting from our men so the soldier bound all the men together and all the women together separately and the children off by themselves. They took all the children, about 50 of us kids, and put us on a bus.

As we rode, I recognized the bridge—it was the same bridge I had crossed into Jordan years before with the Arab man after the bombing of my orphanage house. The bus took us to the same area. About ten soldiers came and got us out and put us on the bridge. No one knew what to do with us. All we knew was we were separated from the tribe. Some of the kids were younger than me and some were older than me. The oldest were teenagers. When we were on the bridge, the soldiers were talking back and forth on walkie-talkies trying to decide where they would send us. Both Jordan and Lebanon were named. They kept talking on the phones. It was getting dark. What were they going to do with us kids? Someone started thanking God.

MY LIFE IN JORDAN

Someone decided to send us to Jordan and Jordan accepted us. So we were on the bus again. It seemed like all night long we were on the bus. Finally they unloaded us, and some women came and hugged us and took us into a building. We found out later that King Hussein himself came and checked on us. One of his relatives had an orphanage and we were placed there. It had running water and was a much better place than my old orphanage. This one was modern. They gave us good food and clothes. They talked to us, asked us our names, and gave us baths.

Since I had been in the desert with the nomads for years, I was really dirty. I had one dress and sandals for summer and winter that were really worn out, so I looked like a homeless child. My hair, which was covered by a scarf, was down to my waist and braided, but we all had lice in our hair. All of our feet were calloused from walking in the desert. We all were in the same condition. These people saw our condition and took care of us. I hadn't been taken care of for years. We were treated like royalty and we stayed there for a long time.

I had learned Islam from the Bedouins, and now in Jordan I continued to live a Muslim life, only no longer in the desert. I was faithful in my belief of the Qur'an and I loved the values that Muhammad taught us. I really didn't have a choice but to love it. It was what I was; it was my life. My entire people believed in the same thing. We were in unity in loving and respecting one another in our culture. Women were taught to work hard and to be respectful to their fathers and to their brothers. I did my prayers. I fasted during Ramadan. I traveled to Mecca, performed *Umrah* and the *Hajj*. I read the Qur'an many times. I looked for God in the Qur'an and I looked for answers. I found some things that brought unity to my life. I loved Allah and I loved Islam very much.

I looked for God in the Qur'an and I looked for answers.

FINDING MY FATHER

I was teenager by now and I was notified by the orphanage that my father had been found and he lived in Jordan. In the orphanage in Israel I had lived with my Jewish family (though not my birth family), and though we spoke Arabic too, we lived as Jews. But when I went to the desert I was called by my first name, and I had only known my first name until then. Now, in Jordan, they had somehow found papers with my real name. At first I was not sure about how accurate this information was but I was told they knew the identity of my mom (who had died after my birth) and the location of my dad who was alive. I thought maybe this could be my chance to no longer be an orphan.

The Jordanian police took me from the orphanage to a town where my father lived. They knocked on the door and told him they had found his daughter. It turns out he had three wives in all—one Iraqi, one Palestinian, and my mother. When they said, "This is your daughter," he denied it. When they told him who my mother was, he said he had never married my mother. So he didn't accept me. The police told him, "It's not your choice," so he had to keep me or the Jordanian police would arrest him. He and his wife took me in, though there was much fighting and cursing going on. He insisted he didn't know who I was. He never accepted me as his child. Instead I became a slave to them.

They knew a man, a relative of my father's wife, who arranged marriages. He lived in New York. He came from New York with a man named Mohammed and his father and his grandmother. They came to Jordan for a wife for Mohammed. He asked for my hand in marriage. I was 15 years old. My father said to me, "This man has come. How would you like to have your own life, your own clothes, your own kitchen? No one will mistreat you." I had 11 brothers and sisters in that family and everyone kicked me and beat me. If I married this man, I'd be free I thought.

So I got married to Mohammed, and I went from Jordan to the United States. The fifth year I got pregnant and had a baby girl. When my daughter was three months old, my husband told me to go visit my family in Jordan. I was hesitant but thought maybe the baby would soften my father's heart.

I went to Jordan with my baby and visited with my father. In the meantime, my husband secretly flew to Jordan after me and divorced me. A police officer came and told my father that my husband had divorced me. They said, because of the law in the States, my daughter would likely have to return to America to her father and the immigration services would be coming to see me. My father became very angry and he was going to kill me because I was a shame to the family as a divorced woman with a child. In Islam, a man can easily divorce his wife if he is unhappy with her, and this usually leaves a cultural stigma of fault and shame on the divorced women.

Somehow, the U.S. Immigration Department sent a person to my father's house, and she insisted that she must talk to me alone. She wore a cross on. She spoke English and full Arabic, which was a good thing as I didn't speak much English even though I had been living in America. She was not covered and clearly not a Muslim. She told my father she needed to talk to me alone. His wife said to my father, "We want to get rid of her. Let her talk to her."

She asked me in Arabic, "If you stay here will you be safe, and will your baby be safe?"

I said, "If I stay they will kill me." It just came out of my mouth.

She said, "I'm taking you back to the United States." She took me and my three-month-old baby and put me on an airplane. She arranged for me to go live with one of my brothers in New York.

When she was nine months old, my ex-husband's family plotted with my father's family and took my child from me and gave her to my ex-husband. One day I came home and saw my sister-in-law bitterly crying because of what just happened. I looked and saw my father put the baby in the back seat of the car and drive off. I was left powerless, in utter shock as a young, traumatized girl. In their mind, taking my daughter was the way they could marry me off to someone else, because it would be harder to be accepted for marriage as a divorced woman with a child.

> *In their mind, taking my daughter was the way they could marry me off to someone else.*

They took her away and I was powerless to do anything about it and afraid they would kill me if I did not accept their plan. I saw her only three times more. I saw her as a young child from afar one time. Then once, many years later, when I was very sick and they thought I would die, they let me see her. Finally, when she became 18 years old, within a year of this writing, she came to see me on Mother's Day.

ABUSED AND ABANDONED

As if losing my daughter wasn't traumatic enough, sure enough the family then told me, "You are being married in a few days." They had arranged a marriage with a man from Libya through the man who arranged my first marriage. No wedding, no party. Nothing. This guy came with a bunch of people I had never met before and took me in a car and moved me to Connecticut. There I had a house with him. We went to the mosque, did the marriage ceremony, and got a marriage certificate. Now I was married again.

I got pregnant on my wedding night and gave birth to a set of twins, a boy and a girl, and then later had another son. My marriage was horrible as my husband would physically beat me and abuse me. He was very cruel. I was afraid of what would happen to me if he hit me one more time. One time he hit me so hard he broke my jaw. I was in the hospital so many times and tried to hide what really happened, and since I did not speak much English I would try to cover up what I was going through.

These problems in the marriage caused me to be very unhappy, but what choice did I have? I focused on being a good mother to my children, and after all I had been through I was not up to losing my children again. We had a house to live in and a place for my children to grow up. I didn't actually hate being a wife, I just hated my husband.

One day he said to me in Arabic, "I'm going to kill you, just like O.J. killed Nicole. I'm going to make sure your face looks worse." At that time, there were many pictures on the television of O.J. Simpson's wife and how she was so badly beaten up and murdered. My husband got really violent with me. He broke my nose. He tore the clothes I was wearing. He had a gun and he shot the gun in the air. Within moments someone was knocking on the door with force. It was police. They arrested him that night and I got taken to the hospital. They took pictures of me. Someone related to me in Arabic, between nurses and doctors and police. They said, "You need to leave before you die like Nicole," the very words my husband had threatened me with.

At that time I heard a voice in my head speaking to me in Arabic saying over and over, "Leave the darkness for the light. Leave the darkness for the light." It was because of the voice that I had the strength to leave that day. I knew I needed to take my children and go.

A lady helped me move our belongings to another area and to rent a house from her relative in a town away from the city I had been living in. When I got there I signed up for welfare, so I got food stamps. I didn't know how to get a job. Other people moved into the house too, so we were sharing the house together. But they were not good people. We had lived there for six months when they took everything away from me and kicked me out onto the street. Later I found out they were drug dealers. Because I didn't know the culture I didn't know what was going on around me. They took my checks, my food stamps, and my house keys. So I was on the street with my three children. We just walked around town, homeless on the streets.

> *They took my checks, my food stamps, and my house keys. So I was on the street with my three children. We just walked around town, homeless on the streets.*

I never took my scarf off, and I said my prayers five times a day. The children spoke English so they translated for me when necessary. We slept in the park. In the mornings we went to a local store to use the bathroom. I looked for nickels and dimes on the ground to buy candy for the children.

Two weeks went by. Everything I owned was still in that house with the drug dealers. I was angry with God. I felt like I wished I could grab the sky and beat up God and then put Him back in the sky. With nothing else to do, I walked back and forth with my children in front of some stores. I often cried and was upset as we walked.

FINDING LOVE FOR THE FIRST TIME

Walking down the street I saw a lady in a shop. I felt so drawn to her store. I finally walked in. The moment I entered, she was very loving and cheerful. She had such nice clothes. I thought, *I have no business being here.* But she received me with so much love, hugging me. I was so puzzled. *What does this woman want from me? I don't even know her name and she's being so loving to me.* It scared me. *Should I trust her? Talk to her?* But I felt drawn to stay.

I said, "I'm looking for a job."

She said, "I know. I will give you a job." She already had seen me in the two weeks I was crossing in front of her store and, as I found out later, she been praying for me. Of course, I had no idea. She was the breaking point for me. She was the *only* person I ever felt the love of God from, though at that time I didn't know it was God's love I was feeling.

I said, "I have no skills, only cooking. I could cook for you."

She said, "Great, I need a cook." And she hired me right then and there—and even with good wages.

We started building a friendship from that moment on. As time went on, our friendship grew deeper and deeper. But something about her puzzled me. *Why does she love me like she does?* When she found out I was homeless, she immediately invited me and my children into her home. Her husband came and got me and my kids and took us into their house and they didn't even charge me. Then she helped me get a place of my own for me and my children.

When I finally asked, she started telling me about Jesus and what she believed. I just interrupted her and told her, "The Qur'an is the truth and Muhammad is the final prophet. Don't say God has a son. That's not to be believed."

> *When she found out I was homeless she immediately invited me and my children into her home.*

She responded, "It's OK to tell me your belief. But can I share my beliefs?" I said OK. She told me about Jesus.

I went back and forth with her. I would tell her, "You are going to hell for your beliefs. We're the true religion. Everyone needs to come to Islam and believe in the last prophet. Our Qur'an teaches God is not a weak God who needs a son. He can help himself. He has no need for a son." I refused what she was saying. "This doesn't make sense," I told her.

She always left me with one sentence: "It's OK to believe what you do. But if you believe in Jesus, He will make your life better."

For two years she told me about Jesus, but because of how I was raised, I couldn't believe God had a son. After all, I was raised with the Qur'an and I loved Muhammad. I wanted to be satisfied like her, but I wasn't. I thought, *I want something of what that woman has.* She didn't have money or great possessions. She had her faith and her faith made her very unique and helpful to every person who came to her store. She greeted them with a smile, a hug, a kiss. She was such a loving person. I wondered, *Is her God like that?* I believed in Allah, but I still had anger and unforgiveness for my family and all I had been through.

When I realized this, I went home and I cried and felt lonely and unsatisfied. She was the opposite. She also went home, and though I knew she had some financial problems, she faced each day with a smile at each new challenge.

Two years went by. I wanted to have her peace and love. I started asking more ways to find out about her faith. I did more fasting, and more Islamic prayers, asking Allah to show up. I prayed, "If you are the truth, why would you not come to me to show me the truth?

LIGHT INSIDE OF LIGHT

One day I was at the store working in the back room. I thought, *Nothing is working. I'm making money but I'm so unhappy. Where is the truth?* Even though He didn't make sense to me, I said, "Jesus, if You are the Son of God, come down and show me." That moment, something started to happen in the room. The room itself changed. All of a sudden a person was standing in front of me, but He was different from any person I'd ever known. I heard His voice, and it was the same voice I heard that had said over and over to me, "Leave the darkness for the light."

He said in Arabic, "I am the Truth, the Life, and the Way, and no one comes to the Father except by Me." He answered in a voice like mighty rushing waters, powerful and soothing at the same time. The minute He said, "I am the Truth," I knew immediately it was Jesus. He hadn't told me that He was Jesus yet, but every fiber of my being knew who He was. I had never read the Bible, but I knew what Jesus was saying to me was in the Bible. I was so consumed by this that I dropped to my knees and looked up at Him. He is so glorious, so beautiful. All light inside of light.

> *All of a sudden a person was standing in front of me, but He was different from any person I'd ever known.*

I said, "Lord! You are Lord!"

He said, "Yes, I am Jesus, the One you denied. The One you said is not the Son of God. I came to save you, to make you a happy person. You don't have to do anything, just know that I love you."

"That's it?" I asked.

He said, "Yes, believe in Me."

It was like I went to school and studied everything in one day. All of a sudden Jesus made sense to me.

He started walking toward me and in a split second He was right there before me. He got so close that there was too much light to see even the color of His eyes, not like you see any other human being. Somehow with His being and His voice came light. A huge light. An overwhelming light. As He was with me for a while, I became part of Heaven. The room was so changed it wasn't the room anymore. I thought, *I am not on earth anymore.* He was talking to me, but at the same time I was seeing Heaven right before my eyes.

Then He said to me, "You are My daughter." The minute the words came out of His mouth they were like living water. I saw everything in one split second and I understood as I saw it all happen. He didn't preach to me, He was just talking to me like another person but with a beautiful and strong voice. It was loving, and sweet like honey. As He got closer, as He was talking to me, it was revealed to me He is the Son of God and He had died on the Cross. I also knew that He is the Lion and the King. It all was revealed to me at once. I also knew the Father in Him and that I was His daughter and His chosen one. All the pain in my life He already knew about, and He was already pleased with me. I knew that all was forgiven by the blood of Jesus.

HEAVEN

As I was seeing right into Heaven, I began to recognize things in Heaven. There was no language barrier. I understood angels were saying,

"Holy, holy, holy." I saw a huge crown and people threw it at the feet of Jesus. I saw children under the age of six and they were all worshiping Jesus. Jesus was speaking to me, explaining things to my mind of what I was seeing. Many of these children were babies who died when their mothers got rid of them through abortion. Some died naturally through sickness or were murdered. All of them were at Jesus' feet and so peaceful and so healthy and happy—not one sad face.

I saw multitudes of people, of every color and race, and I could hear the sounds of every language and tongue. Millions were worshiping Jesus as Lord, calling Him, "Holy, holy Lamb of God" over and over. I saw water, crystal clear water. Everyone was healthy. As I looked at things, I understood them supernaturally. I knew it all by the Spirit of God. I was with the people in Heaven dancing before Jesus, dancing around the throne at His feet. I discovered a place by His feet where I could see the angels, the babies, and the birds of the air. It was all so very beautiful. I was worshiping and calling Him "My God, my Savior, and my King." These things were coming out of my mouth.

> *I saw multitudes of people, of every color and race, and I could hear the sounds of every language and tongue. Millions were worshiping Jesus as Lord, calling Him, "Holy, holy Lamb of God" over and over.*

I was still feeling all this in my body and I was on my knees worshiping Him when Heaven began fading away, though not too quickly. I started sensing I was back on the ground. I could see Jesus backing away in the room. I was still on my knees though I had been standing when He first spoke to me. I was begging Him not to leave me there. "I need You," I told Him, not wanting to ever be without Him again. He said to me in Arabic, "I'm going to come back and get you," He put His hand on me before He left. Right after that, I was flat on the ground and I was back in the room and everything of Heaven faded away.

I got up and sat on my knees. I began to speak in a language I heard in Heaven but never on earth. I had never learned about speaking in tongues.

I saw the Lion in Heaven, the strong Lion. Now as I spoke in that language, I felt that strength inside of me. All of my life of pain, hurt, and sorrow was suddenly before me. It was as if someone took all the pain that had been inside of me and took it out and let me see it and then replaced it with everything that is good. I saw so many negative things before me, but all the good things were there too. I could see both of them, not only the experiences but things in my heart. I recognized them and I was able to choose to replace all the bad with the good. I continued to speak in the heavenly language. I had never used drugs in my life, but I have seen people who were drunk and I was "drunk" with the Spirit of God. I would read later about that happening to the disciples at Pentecost. I felt the weightiness of God on me and yet like I was dancing on a cloud, like I was a bird that could fly in the air.

I walked outside of the room to the front. I was having a hard time walking, still under the weight of the power of His presence. I was not scared for one moment. I felt like I had just been with the love of my life. I knew I could trust that Person. I could trust Him entirely. I now knew who Jesus is. When I walked outside I saw my dear friend and I said to her, "I just received Jesus as my personal Savior. I just talked to Jesus. He's my God and my King." I told her, "He *is* the way and you *do* have to believe in Jesus." I now understood all she had been telling me for two years.

Jesus gave me the love, healing, and security that 29 years in the Qur'an never gave me. Now, by a miracle of the Spirit of God, I was quoting many verses from the Bible though I had never read it. I now knew it is not about us and what we do to try to please God; it's all about Jesus and who He is and what He has done for us! I was filled with the power of Jesus from that day forward. My heart was healed. It was no longer full of hate, anger, confusion, and unforgiveness. I was wholly healed from my childhood as a Palestinian and feeling like a victim of every circumstance. There was such a change in my heart. I wasn't sad anymore. I felt strong, as if I could now face life and any challenges coming before me now that I had Him with me. That's what Jesus provided. He gave me freedom and He gave me love.

> *Jesus gave me the love, healing, and security that 29 years in the Qur'an never gave me.*

COMMENTARY BY FAISAL MALICK

Khalida's life is a message of hope and a powerful example of God's love for everyone. She was orphaned 11 days after birth by the death of her mother. When she was a young girl her orphanage was blown up with a missile, but she was out fetching some water and missed her appointment with death. Then, sold by a man on the street as a slave to the Bedouins, she was raised as a devout Muslim. Abused and beaten in two arranged marriages in a culture where women barely have any rights, her firstborn daughter was taken from her. She finally escaped her second marriage with her remaining three children. A victim of theft by drug dealers and left on the streets as a single mom, she remained faithful to her beliefs in Islam and to Allah until she encountered Jesus in person. She experienced Heaven and came to the revelation that God is Father. She finally met the Truth and realized that Jesus is the Son of God, which she previously denied as a Muslim.

Khalida realized so much so quickly in her heavenly experience, but one of the most important things we can take away from her story is the love she experienced in Jesus. This love healed her of all her hatred, bitterness, and abuse and made her a new person full of love. God's love can heal the deepest wounds and change the most impossible circumstances. Real love is the very essence of God. God is love and Jesus is the ultimate expression of that love.

> *He who does not love does not know God, for God is love* (1 John 4:8).

Once you experience Jesus and you surrender your heart to Him, then the very essence of His light will overwhelm your soul and cleanse you from sin. You will experience God's love.

I do not know your journey in life or what you have been through, but I do know that God loves you and that it is not too late for hope in the midst of your life. The sufferings of this present world are not worthy to be compared with the beauty that shall be revealed in you one day. No matter how difficult your life has been or how scarred your soul, God can heal your wounds and make you new. Love will make you more than a conqueror in life.

> No matter how difficult your life has been or how scarred your soul, God can heal your wounds and make you new. Love will make you more than a conqueror in life.

The greatest demonstration of love is Jesus coming from Heaven to earth and dying for you on the Cross so you could be forgiven and so God's wrath against your sin would be satisfied, allowing you to have a relationship with God. You only have one life to live and it counts for eternity.

Remember the powerful words of Jesus:

> ...*I am the way, the truth, and the life. No one comes to the Father except through Me* (John 14:6).

If you are ready to give your life to Jesus and experience this true love, then pray this prayer with me.

> *Jesus, I surrender my life to You and I want know this magnificent love. I believe You are the Way, the Truth, and the Life. Reveal the Father to me and show me Your love. I believe You are the Word of God and You came to earth and became Man to die for me on the Cross. I believe You rose again from the dead and You are Lord.*

CHAPTER 5

DELIVERANCE FROM DEMONS AND DRUGS

Güçlü (Corey) Erman

AS A YOUNG BOY BORN and raised in a Muslim family in Ankara, Turkey, I had a great hunger for the things of God. Even as a child I wanted to know about God. I practiced Islam as I was taught, praying five times a day, and I went to the mosque with my grandfather on Fridays. One day, when I was ten years old, my grandfather rebuked me for showing emotion at the mosque. Something broke in me that day that would not be healed for many years.

When I was 13 years old we immigrated to the United States. Not knowing anyone, I was so lonely that I gave myself more to religion. I did everything I could to fill the emptiness inside. At around 15 or 16, with that emptiness still deep inside of me, I began to wonder about what I was doing. I had memorized the Arabic prayers in the Qur'an and said them five times a day, but being Turkish speaking, and later speaking English, I really didn't understand what I was praying. I did it only out of my religious duty. The repetitious prayers left me empty and without any understanding of what I was praying. It became so unfulfilling, especially after some of the things I heard at Friday prayers.

WHY THE HATRED?

I began to question why there was so much such hatred. There was always hatred imparted in the messages in Islam. Even from early childhood I heard hatred for Christians, and as a Turk I especially heard hatred for Armenians and Greeks. One day, while I was at Friday noon prayer at the Islamic Center in Baton Rouge, Louisiana, a lot of hatred for America and Israel was being preached. That day I made a decision not to go back to the mosque. I was looking for peace and love. This hatred was not what I wanted in my life. I loved being in America. I couldn't understand why they lived there but yet they hated it. So I stopped going to the mosque and I stopped praying and practicing Islam. But this did not change the emptiness inside—I still had the emptiness. So as a teen trying to make friends, I started partying, smoking marijuana, taking drugs, and even taking ecstasy pills. It was all crazy.

I SAW THE FLAMES OF HELL

Someone invited me to a "house party." I thought it was a "real" party. When I got there, kids were sitting on the floor. Someone turned out the lights and another teen started to pray. All of a sudden, I started crying. I didn't know why, but I was so embarrassed that I left and did the only thing I knew to do. I went around the corner to find some other guys to smoke marijuana with.

> I was sitting on the floor early in the morning hours in a club when I heard an audible voice. The voice said, "Get up. You will never be this way again."

One night I was really high on drugs. I was sitting on the floor early in the morning hours in a club when I heard an audible voice. The voice said, "Get up. You will never be this way again." The voice was like a loud voice coming from inside. I don't know to this day if I heard it in my mind or if I actually heard it audibly. But it was loud and clear to me at the time. At that very moment, I immediately came to myself, the effect of the drugs completely left me, and I was entirely clear-minded. At the same time, I was convicted in my heart so deeply at the sound of the voice that I knew I was in sin. I had no concept of salvation. In Islam we know of sin and hell, but not of salvation. You're always trying to earn your way to salvation but you're never sure of attaining it. So I thought, *I have committed the unpardonable sin and I'm going to hell.*

At that same moment, I actually saw the flames of hell. It seemed like the flames were in the room and also somehow in my future. I didn't see hell itself, but I knew the flames represented hell. I also saw ugly demonic creatures sitting on people's shoulders, and I knew the demons (called *jinn* by Muslims) were controlling the people—including me—through the drugs. It terrified me. I got up like the voice had told me, and as fast as I could, I left that place. Even though I never went back there, for years afterward I struggled with demons. Some tried to suffocate me in my sleep and other demons jumped on me and put their claws in my body. I actually felt the excruciating physical pain of it. I also had unclean dreams. My party friends and I had seen and done many strange things when under the influence of drugs, which opened me up to these demons, and I continued to deal with their activity in my life.

I tried to reform my life. In religion you try self-reformation. I tried to become a good person and to live a good life. I quit all my relationships with those friends. I knew there was a God out there whom I didn't know. I was feeling very guilty. I questioned constantly what was to happen with my life and my eternal state. Not long after this, I moved away to college in Texas.

I had a scholarship that would be renewable every year. I had fulfilled all the requirements for the second year when I received a letter in the mail that my scholarship was not going to be renewed. It was a shock to me. I was going through such a bad time as it was already. My family had no money to cover the cost for college. I really needed this scholarship. I was crying and weeping, I was so discouraged. As I went to my dorm room, I bumped into a guy who always had this peace on his face. Now I know it was a divine appointment.

PRAYING FOR A MIRACLE

He took one look at me and asked, "Are you OK?" I told him I was going through a hard time. He asked me if I wanted to talk, so we went and sat in my dorm room, and for the first time in my life someone shared the *Injil* (Gospel) with me, telling me that Jesus Christ died on a Cross for my sins. He drew a picture of sinful man and a holy God with a huge gap in between the two. I knew that was my case. I had tried through religion but I could not reach God. In fact, I thought that I may have offended God so much that He really hated me. I was very confused about it. But now this guy was telling me of a God who really loves me and about salvation, that I could be saved not only from my sin, but also from an eternity in hell. He told me if I believed that Jesus died on the Cross, God would forgive me and wash me and cleanse me of all my sin and give me a new beginning in life.

My Muslim head was fighting with what he was saying because we had been taught that Jesus didn't really die on the Cross and that He is not the Son of God. I was arguing in my mind, but in my heart I was so hungry for a reality of God. Because of all the knowledge I had learned previously, I was stuck. Not knowing what else to say, I said, "I'm a Muslim."

He said, "I don't want to argue with you. Can I just pray for you? Can I just bless you?" I said yes. I needed prayer so much.

I thought he would begin to speak in Latin and do the sign of the Cross over me, or go and get some holy water or from the tap and sprinkle it on my head. That was my concept of Christianity. He put his hands on my shoulder and began to pray that God would give me a miracle, that He would show me His grace and love, that He would bless me and help me. And he prayed that God would help me to stay in school. A peace came over me. It was such a peace, I felt almost drunk. It was an amazing peace like I had never known before. I just felt that everything was going to be OK. He left and I never saw him again. Within one week I had not one miracle but two.

Within one week I had not one miracle but two.

First, I got a letter from the college saying that they were sorry they made a mistake about the scholarship and they were going to *double it!* And second, someone—I don't even know who—connected me with an elderly couple who were alumni of the school who wanted to meet me. They said someone was going to give me *another scholarship.* They invited me to lunch, and before we ate they held hands and bowed their heads and began to pray. I didn't know what to do, so I held their hands and bowed my head. These people who didn't even know me began to pray blessings over me. I felt such love coming from these strangers. In my loneliness God was reaching out to me and was becoming real to me. Occasionally, I began to go to some Christian meetings on campus. Someone would play the guitar and someone would read from the Bible and pray. The love I felt from these people was beginning to open my heart which had been closed to Christianity from the time I was a little boy so many years before.

One night I went outside to the park and reached my arms to the sky and I cried out to God, "I know You are out there somewhere. Who are You? Show Yourself to me. Are you Muhammad? Are You Jesus?" That night I had a powerful dream of someone being raised from the dead. The dream was really simple. A dead man was lying there very hopeless. I was looking at him and all of a sudden he stood up. It was almost scary the way he came back to life. I just thought, *Wow, the man came back to life!* I pondered that dream. Through this whole process, one incident at a time, God was touching my heart.

Then a friend and my roommate came to me and told me that he had become a Christian. I thought that was strange since he was already a Christian. He told me that he was Catholic, but he had just been born again. I had never heard that before. When he talked about Jesus, his eyes filled up with tears of joy. It was so real to him. His experience was so real to him that I asked him to take me to church and I started attending church with him. That Sunday, the pastor preached from Genesis chapter 1 about *me* being made in the image of God and that God has a special plan and purpose for each of us. He said that I would not be fulfilled until I discovered this plan. That message touched me deeply.

COMPASSION AND FORGIVENESS

One day I came home to find my roommate sitting on his bed and his eyes were bloodshot. He told me how a boyfriend had raped his sister and he wanted to go and shoot him. But he had been praying all morning and was finally able to forgive him and pray for his salvation. I was so full of hatred and unforgiveness, I thought, *How could he forgive this guy who raped his sister?* I was so angry at many people for hurting me. My previous roommate had cheated me out of a lot of money and I could not forgive him, but this guy was able to forgive the man who raped his sister! He was crying and I heard the compassion in his voice and I was so convicted by his ability to forgive.

He reached out to me and he said, "Man, are you ready to meet Jesus?" He had been praying for me for a while, I found out later. It was obvious I was a very angry and bitter person. We had talked about some of these things before, but seeing how I reacted to his compassion and forgiveness, he felt compelled to pray with me. I don't even know what really happened, except that I grabbed his hand and closed my eyes and the next thing I knew he was leading me in this prayer. I was praying something like: "Jesus, come into my heart, be my Lord, forgive me for all my sins, cleanse me, change me." He said, *amen* and I said *amen*.

I BECOME A NEW PERSON

When I opened my eyes I felt like a completely brand-new person. I remember looking around the room and saying, "Everything is so bright. Did you paint the room?" It was as if a darkness that had surrounded me was gone. The trees outside looked so alive. Everything was so alive! I felt so excited. A great weight had lifted off of my shoulders. And all the guilt was gone. I remember thinking, looking in the mirror, *Did I just become a*

Christian? Yes, I became a Christian. It felt so good to say it. I became born again instantly with a true consciousness of the peace of Jesus Christ, and that day, I began my adventure with God.

Within months there was a radical change in my life. The Lord set me free from all kinds of bondage and anger. I had a lot of insecurity and fears. He began to make me whole. My prayer times were so amazing. I wanted to pray all the time and read my Bible. I just wept in His Presence and His love and tenderness were so real to me. I felt His touch. I got so much revelation from reading His Word. As a result, some of my friends realized the reality of Jesus. So did my mom and my sister too. My father at first was speechless and angry, but later God touched him in a powerful way. (See Hamdi Erman's story in this book.)

Jesus was so wonderful to me. I realized that I had so many curses on my life. God began to set me free from so many dark and unclean things. During this time I was completely set free from all the demonic (*jinn*) torments that had been in my life from the drugs. I became full of joy and passion for God. I could rest in His love for me now that I understood that I couldn't earn salvation. It wasn't about what I did, but what Jesus did when He died to pay the price of sin. The only thing I had to do was receive it from Him.

A VISION CHANGES MY FUTURE

In November 1995, I had a very supernatural encounter. Jesus appeared to me and summoned me to serve Him and become a minister of the *Injil* (Gospel). Let me explain what happened. After college I began working in Houston, Texas for a consulting firm. I had a great job, but inside I felt that there must be so much more for me to do. I began to seek God about this in my prayer times.

> *Jesus appeared to me and summoned me to serve Him and become a minister of the Injil.*

One day I had come from the office and returned to my apartment around 3:30 in the afternoon. I was sitting on the couch when all of a sudden I felt something come into the room. It felt like a wave of God's Presence (now I know it was the glory of God). The atmosphere of the room changed. It came from the far end toward me and hit my feet. It went right through me like a warm and tingly feeling. When it went through my head, instantly I was in a vision or a dream—I'm not sure what to call it. I was standing by the seashore. I went into the water, which was ankle deep. I was trying to hold the water in the palms of my hands, but it would just roll off. A strong but compassionate voice spoke out of Heaven and said, "This is Islam, and there is no truth to hold on to."

Then suddenly I found myself in the middle of the ocean in a terrible storm. The waves were crashing over me. It was dark and so scary. I was trying to stay up, but I kept swallowing water and I was sinking into what seemed like a deep abyss. I felt what it is like to be lost without hope. I had no chance to make it. But somehow I knew this was the feeling others feel in Turkey and their eternal destiny. It was as if God was making me feel this, or reminding me of it. I was crying out for help, and suddenly someone (I never saw him) picked me up from the back of my neck and lifted me up from the water. I kept being carried up into the sky. I came through the storm into bright, quiet skies. It kept getting brighter as we kept going higher. Then I was dropped off on top of the clouds.

I was trying to look but it was so bright I couldn't see. I was standing on a cloud. Suddenly I saw the Lord Jesus coming down from above toward the cloud on which I stood. He came so fast and stood right in front of me. He almost touched the cloud, but stood just a foot above it. Somehow I realized He is coming back so very soon. The Bible tells us that when He returns to the earth, He will come through the clouds. The vision showed me that His coming will be on the clouds, but He hasn't yet touched them. He never said a word, but He stood in front of me and held His hands out to me. His face was shining as brightly as the noonday sun. His hair was like flames of fire in the wind, but there was no wind. He had a white glowing garment on Him all the way down to His ankles. A gold diagonal sash lay on His chest. His eyes looked like they pierced me and also looked past me. I knew instantly that He wanted me to give my life to the service of the Gospel and sharing it with the Muslims. It may sound like all this took a while, but it felt instantaneous. When He came and stood near me, I realized all of these things. I took one look at Him, but I could not bear to look at Him out of fear of His holiness and power, and I fell at His feet.

> *I took one look at Him, but I could not bear to look at Him out of fear of His holiness and power, and I fell at His feet.*

When I came out of the vision, I was on my face in the living room and shaken by the experience. I felt so weak physically. When I could finally gather myself after a few minutes, I looked out the window and it was dark. I looked at my watch and it was 9:30 P.M. Six hours had passed by in what seemed like a 30-second vision. That day God broke my heart for the people of Turkey. I had no intention of ever going back. I hated so many things about Turkey. But I couldn't sleep for days. I just wept and prayed for the nation and the people. They were lost and I had a sense that I was responsible for it. I knew I had to share the good news of Jesus with them.

A CONFIRMING DREAM

I had a dream one night shortly after this experience and found myself overlooking a city. I recognized the landmark castle on top of a hill as I was floating over it. It was the castle in Ulus, Ankara. The same voice I had heard before said, "This is the city of your birth." I looked out to the city, and normally you would just see a sea of buildings. But I saw the whole land filled with tombstones and there was an eerie calm and darkness. The voice said, "They are all dying. You must tell them the Gospel of life."

Within a month I resigned my career. I sold or gave away most of my things and moved back to Turkey with two suitcases. I didn't know of any other Christians, any churches, etc. I only had some extended family there. But God equipped me with what I needed. Shortly after I arrived in

Turkey, the Lord baptized me with His fire one night to start this ministry. I felt fire all over my body, soul, and spirit. This was not the fire of hell; this was the fire of God and His glory! It was a powerful experience that lasted for about 45 minutes, then subsided to where I could still feel it for a while. A "baptism of fire" is the baptism of the Holy Spirit and fire that John the Baptist talked about and that Jesus spoke of as recorded in the Bible in the Book of Acts. It is what the disciples received on the day of Pentecost. What happened to them happened to me—the infilling of the Holy Spirit with the evidence of speaking in other tongues (see Acts 2:4; Matt. 3:11; Luke 3:16).

When it happened to the disciples, they were able to do the same miracles that Jesus had done. A few days later I prayed for a Muslim girl with a golf ball-sized tumor on her neck. The minute I touched her she screamed out saying my hand burned her—she felt the fire of God—and the tumor entirely disappeared! It's been like that ever since on hundreds of occasions. As I write this, it has been 14 years that I have dedicated my life full-time to ministry in Turkey, preaching the Gospel to the Muslims as God confirms His Word with signs and wonders and miracles and brings many into the assurance of His love, now and forever.

> *I prayed for a Muslim girl with a golf ball-sized tumor on her neck. The minute I touched her she screamed out saying my hand burned her—she felt the fire of God—and the tumor entirely disappeared!*

COMMENTARY BY FAISAL MALICK

Corey's journey toward God began with a dream. In the mind of a Muslim, since the time of the death of Muhammad, the final prophet of Islam, a dream or a vision is one of the only ways God can still speak to people. Often God uses a dream to communicate with our hearts and give us clues about our future. Not every dream we have is from God, but He does use the language of dreams to speak to us. When a dream is from

God it always inspires in us hope, even when it is a warning. Growing up as a Muslim I remember how in my family we always paid close attention to our dreams. We tried to interpret and draw out the meaning of the dreams and we wondered if there was some kind of direction or answer found in the dream pertaining to our lives.

Let me share a powerful truth that was revealed to the prophet David as recorded in the *Zabur* (Book of Psalms), which is part of the third book Muslims believe came from Heaven.

> *Your eyes saw my substance, being yet unformed. And in Your book they all were written, the days fashioned for me, when as yet there were none of them* (Psalm 139:16).

Did you know that God wrote a book about you before you were even born? It includes His thoughts, design, and perspectives about who you are, your past, your future—your ultimate destiny. He saw you even before you were formed, and He wrote about your potential before your life even began.

Have you ever wondered why a certain circumstance, experience, sentence in a book, statement, or dream so impacts you? You never seem to forget it or stop thinking about it, or it gives you an overwhelming desire to seek for answers. Often these promptings lead you to something you would have never expected. Such moments are part of the divine tapestry of God's plan for your life. In that particular moment your heart is connecting with something God wrote about you before you were born—a piece of the puzzle about your destiny. In those special moments God is trying to speak to you about the hidden things and secrets reserved for your life regardless of your spiritual state. That is why moments like these capture your heart. When Jesus appeared to Corey, his heart melted for the people of Turkey. As Corey noticed those divine moments on his path, God kept moving him closer to his destiny.

> *Your heart is connecting with something God wrote about you before you were born—a piece of the puzzle about your destiny.*

Your destiny may be very different from Corey's, but it begins with you recognizing and cultivating the "God moments" in your life. God cares for you and sees you right where you are. He is pleased with the spiritual hunger in your heart and your desire to know and obey Him. You may be sensing the presence of Jesus and becoming aware of His love for you. He is the source of all the forgiveness and healing you are looking for. As you continue to read these stories, you will find special moments in which you will connect with God through the lives of these people whom God has touched.

> *Father, I pray that You pour Your Spirit on this person and speak to him or her in dreams and visions and reveal Your plans and purpose for his life. May he know Your holy Presence all the days of his life.*

CHAPTER 6

GOD IS LIGHT
Hamdi Erman

MY NAME IS HAMDI ERMAN. I am a 66-year-old Turkish man at the writing of this book. I was born and raised in Ankara, Turkey. My family was Muslim and my father taught me about the Islamic religion. Even as a child I was really focused on my practice of Islam. When I was in elementary school, my dad took me to a mosque to learn and study the Qur'an. During summers Qur'an courses were always held for the kids to learn how to practice Islam. They always kept the boys and girls in separate rooms. Every Friday my dad took me to midday prayer whenever I was at home. Going to a mosque on Fridays, which is a holy day for Islam, became a habit.

In 1969 I got married to someone who had very little religious experience in her life. As long as she was Turkish, my father didn't ask whether she was a practicing Muslim or not or say anything about my wife, because he was not a fanatical man in his beliefs. My parents were more open-minded people than many others. My wife and I had two children, first a boy and then later a girl.

I MOVED TO AMERICA FOR BUSINESS

In 1980, we decided to move to the United States for business purposes. Years later I realized that this was all part of God's plan. In America I tried never to miss my times of prayer in order to be a good Muslim. My father had told me when we were moving to the States, "Do not let your children lose their faith. Teach them everything." That was his concern. Our daughter knew less about our faith than our son. He was different because he had some background while we were still living in Turkey. In the U.S., I continued teaching him and instructing him to practice our faith. I thought Islam was the best religion in the world. It was very important to me for my children to know our faith.

When I was new to the United States, I assumed the whole country would be Christian so I really wanted to protect my son from too much Christian influence and raise him up as a good Muslim.

MY SON BECOMES A CHRISTIAN

While my son was in college, his roommate began sharing the message of Jesus with him. He even took him to his church. Through a sequence of events, over time my son had become a Christian. One day he called his mom and told her that he chose to become a Christian. As I mentioned before, my wife had little to no Muslim background so she wasn't against our son's new choice. She was listening to him very seriously and keeping it a secret from me. She knew what my response would be.

When my son finally shared this with me, I got very upset and angry with him. How could he do this to our family? How could he violate my faith? I thought his friends had brainwashed him. All his life, I had taught him to grow up as a good Muslim man. Now he failed me. To make things worse, he was telling me all these conflicts and inconsistencies with Islam, which made me even angrier. I was also worried about how to explain all this to my mother and relatives back in Turkey (my dad was already dead). Both my parents had gone to Mecca a few times. They also did the pilgrimage trips to Mecca for my deceased grandparents. So how could I possibly tell my mother and relatives my son was now a Christian? That would be such a disgrace to them and this troubled me more.

> All his life, I had taught him to grow up as a good Muslim man. Now he failed me.

I tried to reason with my son, and I had some long talks on the telephone with him too. In the end I hid his conversion from my relatives back home and decided to leave him alone. I said to him, "If this is going to make you happy, then OK." After all, he was an adult who could make his own choices.

JESUS IS AFFECTING MY FAMILY

My son now lived in Houston, Texas and was doing well in a prestigious career and for that I was happy. He would call my wife every night reading to her from the Bible about Jesus. Before I knew it, Jesus was affecting my family. During Christmas my wife and my daughter chose the Christian faith also. All this was a shock to me. I thought, *Everybody is leaving me!* That's how I felt. Abandoned. My confusion was growing and I kept asking, "Why? Why?"

One day my son called me with more shocking news. He told me he was going to quit his career and life in America and go to Turkey to do God's work! This idea made me more upset. *My son went to a good college and earned a good degree. He has a good job and is being paid a good salary. Now he is blowing off his future and moving to Turkey? Besides, when he's in Turkey, my family will learn about his Christianity if he tells them. I have an elderly mother. What if something happens to her when she hears it?* All these things were coming to my mind.

After some very long talks, I finally said OK because nothing was going to change his vision. He was not even really asking my permission. He had already made up his mind. My concern was what my relatives and my elderly mother were going to think. But I knew if I told him not to go, he wouldn't listen anyway. He was that sure about God's call on his life. How was I to argue with that?

I went to Houston to take some of my son's personal things to him and to say goodbye. We were living in Tampa, Florida at the time. When I went to meet with him we had long talks again. He gave me some teaching tapes to listen to while driving back home. He took me to his church on Sunday. Everybody welcomed me and many said, "We're praying for you, Mr. Erman." I never had anyone tell me that before. They were praying for me? In Islam, people don't pray for others they don't know. This was entirely new to me.

> They were praying for me? In Islam, people don't pray for others they don't know. This was entirely new to me.

NOW JESUS IS AFFECTING ME!

I listened to the tapes while I was driving back home and got more confused. I had never heard these things in Islam. The person on the tapes was talking about God's love. In Islam God is not love. He punishes and gives the impression of being an angry God. This man was saying that God loves the sinners. That if we stay away from fleshly desires, God promises a peaceful life. The moment I heard those words, conviction came on me that I was not a good person. I was a sinner. Islam doesn't tell you that you are a sinner. I liked worldly music and drinking a little alcohol. Yes, drinking is forbidden in Islam, but I was not really following that rule. Not all Muslim people do what they are supposed to do all the time. Some observe the holy days like Ramadan and Eid and go back to the same old lifestyle after that. I remembered all these things as I listened to the tape, and I almost hated myself because of my own sin.

One evening I came home from work after working long hours. My wife was in Turkey for a business purpose and my daughter was in college in another town. So I was all alone at home.

I was still thinking about a solution to find out what to believe. My mind was racing and my desperation to find answers was rising up on the inside. Everything was changing suddenly and unusual things were happening. For 14 years in the States, no one talked to me and my wife about Jesus. All of a sudden I began hearing all these things about Jesus. What was happening? I had always believed that Jesus was one of the prophets, but Muhammad was the last prophet and the Qur'an was the last holy book. That's what I was told all the years of my life. I didn't know enough about Jesus to compare him with Muhammad. Nor could I compare the Bible and Qur'an. Like any good Muslim, I had memorized the prayers and scriptures from the Qur'an in Arabic, but since I spoke Turkish, I memorized them without knowing what the words actually said.

A BRIGHT LIGHT FILLED THE ROOM

I decided to forget it all for a while and watch sports on television. I was clicking the remote but it was not working. It was not moving at all, and then it jumped to another channel. All of a sudden I saw a man talking, and he pointed his finger at me through the television screen and said, "There is a man right now who is very confused about what is going on around him. God loves you so much and He is your answer." Suddenly an awe of God came over me. I knelt down in my living room and said, "I don't know what to do; I am so overwhelmed. If You are really God talking to me You have to prove it to me." I was talking to God, asking Him to show Himself to me if He was real. I didn't mention the name of Jesus; I would have been afraid to use His name.

Suddenly a huge bright light filled the room. As I looked up, a man was standing there, but He was so bright, like the brightness of the sun, that it was hard to see. He was very close to my face so that my eyes weren't able to see anything. I could see His white garment, but I couldn't see His face that was shining so brightly. It was very hard to understand at that time what I was seeing, but I know now that it was God's glory that was shining in the room.

He touched my right shoulder and said with an audible voice, "Hamdi, just follow Me." Jesus was standing before me! His voice was so soft, like velvet. He had heard my prayer and He answered me by coming to my room to prove Himself to me! I knew something incredibly special was happening. My heart was pounding, but I was not afraid because I knew He was Jesus. Jesus was standing in my living room with such love, and when He spoke to me it was with such a loving voice. I had asked that He prove Himself to me and here He was in front of me, real and alive, talking to me. And He—Jesus—was inviting me to follow Him.

I don't know how much time I spent in His presence, but when I came to myself I was on the other side of the house in my daughter's room on the carpet. I was crying, laughing, and saying some words but I didn't understand. It was not English or Turkish. I was shaking when I came to myself. When I looked at my watch it was 3:00 A.M. I kept thinking, *Jesus came to visit me!* He answered my prayer. He came to my life. He touched me, He saved me, and He baptized me all at the same time. He had baptized me in the Holy Spirit and I was speaking in a language unknown to me, although I didn't know then that I had experienced the baptism of the Holy Spirit and was speaking heavenly tongues. I only knew that He had come to me and changed me. His fire was still burning on my body. I knew He saved me right there and filled me with His Holy Spirit and fire.

In the morning I visited the pastor of the church that my wife was attending and told him the story. He told me that I had a very special visitation that most people would love to have. I knew I was saved the night before, but I had to share the experience with the pastor. I made the decision to follow and serve Jesus for the rest of my life.

MY FAMILY RESPONDS

When I called my wife and son in Turkey the first thing I said was, "I am waiting for you for my water baptism."

Both of them were in shock. They started shouting "Hallelujah!" and dancing. I knew how happy they would be.

> *When I called my wife and son in Turkey the first thing I said was, "I am waiting for you for my water baptism."*

But I have to tell you about my mother's reaction. When my son and my wife went to visit the family, of course they told her everything. She wasn't very much worried about them, but when she heard about me becoming a believer in Jesus, she was very upset. When I called her on the phone from America she cursed me and disowned me. She also kicked my son out of her home because he shared Jesus with his cousins. For five years my mother never spoke to me on the phone. My older sister, who was divorced, and her two sons were living with my mother. My sister was willing to still speak with me. Every time I called, my sister said that either my mother was in the bathroom or praying or doing something else. I kept asking my sister to tell my mother that I loved her.

My wife and I went to visit Turkey for a short trip and ended up living there permanently. In Turkey I met with my mother on special occasions like weddings and a celebration for my nephew's newborn baby. On those visitations my mother allowed me to kiss her. I was praying every day for her heart to be softened. Finally she asked me to come home to visit her. That was a breakthrough. I went to visit there very often after that over the next few years. My sister and my brother finally accepted us because they recognized the many positive changes in us as a result of knowing Jesus.

At one point my mother let me pray for her knees, which I did by laying hands on her and praying in Jesus' name. She knew when I prayed something different was happening to her, especially once she was able to go to the restroom on her own without help. Three years passed and she had breast cancer at the age of 93, which was very unusual for someone of that age. One of her breasts was removed and the doctors said the cancer wouldn't come back. But it came back when she was 97 years old. My wife and I wife were visiting our daughter in the States when I heard this news. I rushed back to my mother's town to see her. She had a big tumor on her neck. I laid hands on her neck and prayed in Jesus' name, and in a few days the tumor was gone. Another time my mother broke her leg and had an operation and pins were put in. She was in a coma for three days. I prayed in her ears that Jesus loved her. She survived that coma and lived about four more weeks.

> *My mom didn't realize that the person in light was Jesus, but she made the choice even in her dream to respond to the One who is light.*

One day I was alone in the room with her and I said, "Mom, Jesus is your Healer and your Savior." I led her in repeating a very short prayer. A few days after this prayer, she told my sister that when she was sleeping two men came in the room. One was wearing dark clothes and was very handsome. He told her to come. She looked at him and refused him and pushed him aside. The other one was all in white and shining very brightly. He also called her to go with Him. When she woke up, she told my sister that an angel called her to go and the time was coming. She didn't realize that the person in light was Jesus, but she made the choice even in her dream to respond to the One who is light. A few days later she died in her sleep. I rest assured that my mother is with Jesus.

JESUS HEALS ME

Jesus also healed me from my allergies and asthma attacks. Two years after I got saved, our church was going to have a special healing service one Sunday evening. Our pastor told us to prepare our hearts to receive healing. I was ready. I had allergies and asthma for about 40 years, and I had spent a lot of money on them but with no results. When the pastor called people to the front for prayer, I ran. When he laid hands on me, I fell to the floor under the power of God. I felt like a big oxygen tank blew up in my lungs. I knew Jesus had opened up my lungs. About 11 years have passed since then. I can smell a good perfume or a fragrant candle. In the past I couldn't do that without sneezing or getting a runny nose and eyes. Forty years of sickness—yet with one prayer, Jesus healed me.

My whole family is now serving the Lord, including my daughter and my son-in-law. I live in Istanbul with my wife and my son and his family. I am serving at the church as an ordained pastor. I took Jesus' great commission to tell others about Him as my personal call. I am reaching out to those who are lost without Him and sharing the Gospel with every person I meet. I have a great love and compassion for my country. Jesus gave that love to me. God has a plan and purpose for the Muslim people.

> *I heard many, many times as a Muslim that God would punish me if I did the things he doesn't like. God is not like that. He loves us. He is our friend. He cries with us or is happy with us. He is our helper, and He guides us.*

This is what I have to tell my Muslim friends: The love I received from God is greater than anything I received during all my Muslim years. The touch of God is very different. God can touch you. The fear of God is totally different. He is not a punisher. I heard many, many times as a Muslim that God would punish me if I did the things he doesn't like. God is not like that. He loves us. He is our friend. He cries with us or is happy with us. He is our helper, and He guides us. God is not in a box; He is out there with us, in us, and for us. You have just read that He talked to me. He will talk with you. He is the knowable God! And most of all, God loves you!

COMMENTARY BY FAISAL MALICK

Many Muslims around the world recite the Qur'an in Arabic but do not know the meaning of what they are saying or praying. Jesus in the *Injil* warned us that meaningless repetitions of prayer would not get an audience with God (see Matt. 6:7). Hamdi was no different in his Islamic approach to God, being Turkish and unable to understand Arabic. It was only when he humbled himself and sincerely talked to God that the deepest questions of his heart were answered.

> Many Muslims around the world recite the Qur'an in Arabic but do not know the meaning of what they are saying or praying.

God is light, and that is why when Hamdi saw Jesus, he saw bright light that filled his room. This encounter with Jesus overwhelmed him with God's holy Presence and fire and left him speaking in an unknown heavenly language. This experience can also be yours as promised by God through John the Baptist, one of the most important prophets recognized by both Muslims and Christians alike. John the Baptist prophesied about the coming of Jesus who would baptize us with the Holy Spirit and fire.

> *...I indeed baptize you with water; but One mightier than I is coming, whose sandal strap I am not worthy to loose. He* [Jesus] *will baptize you with the Holy Spirit and fire* (Luke 3:16).

Let's gain a further understanding of God's holy fire and Presence by reading the biblical account of the prophet Ezekiel who saw God seated on His throne:

> *And above the firmament over their heads was the likeness of a throne, in appearance like a sapphire stone; on the likeness of the throne was a likeness with the appearance of a man high above it. Also from the appearance of His waist and upward I saw, as it were, the color of amber*

> *with the appearance of fire all around within it; and from*
> *the appearance of His waist and downward I saw, as it*
> *were, the appearance of fire with brightness all around.*
> *Like the appearance of a rainbow in a cloud on a rainy*
> *day, so was the appearance of the brightness all around it.*
> *This was the appearance of the likeness of the glory of the*
> *Lord...* (Ezekiel 1:26-28).

Notice in the above verses that Ezekiel saw on the throne the appearance of a man with fire from His waist upward and fire and brightness downward. The fire is a visible manifestation of the glory of God. When you see Jesus you see and experience His mighty Presence as holy fire. This is the fire in which God called out to Moses from the burning bush. The prophet Ezekiel saw the fire of God in Heaven in the appearance like that of a man on the throne. Ezekiel saw Jesus on the throne. That is why the Bible says that God was manifest in the flesh—it is referring to Jesus coming to earth and taking on a human body.

James, Peter, and John, three disciples of Jesus, saw Him transfigured into His glorious bright state while He was on earth (see Matt. 17:1-8). After Jesus ascended back to Heaven, John saw Jesus again in a vision while on the Isle of Patmos. Jesus' face was shining brighter than the sun and fire was coming out of His eyes (see Rev. 1:14-16). Jesus is holy, the express image of God's being and the brightest expression of His glory. Jesus is alive and willing to baptize with His Spirit and fire.

When the prophet Isaiah was before the throne of God, an angel first touched his lips with the coals of fire and then God commissioned him to speak to the people (see Isa. 6:6-8.) That is a spiritual blueprint and prophetic picture of what happens to you when you get baptized with the Holy Spirit and fire. You begin to speak in a new language like Hamdi did. The only way to experience this is to know Jesus.

There is more potential to your life than you may realize. Jesus came to earth to die for you and shed His blood for you and for your sins, and then He arose from the dead to the right hand of God ever ready to baptize you with His Holy Spirit and fire.

Your journey begins with the same simple instruction Jesus gave to Hamdi—"Follow Me." If you sense the gentle tug in your heart to follow Jesus, then pray this prayer with me and ask Him to baptize you with His Spirit and with fire.

Let's pray:

> *God, I desire to have a meaning full relationship with You and follow You all the days of my life. I desire to hear Your voice and know You. Jesus, I believe You are the Light and I surrender my life to You right now. I confess You are God manifest in the flesh and You died for me and rose again from the dead. You are the answer to all my questions and I ask You to baptize me with Your Holy Spirit and fire now. Amen.*

CHAPTER 7

SHOW ME THE WAY
Cemil and Isil Akbulut

MY NAME IS CEMIL. I was born and raised in Turkey. My parents died when I was a child so I was raised by my older brother. When I was nine years of age, he used to take me to the mosque for *Namaz,* to pray five times a day in the Islamic religious tradition. He was a very religious man and he raised me to be religious like himself. Our house was full of Islamic religious books.

While I was growing up I got involved in Islamic cults, first with *Naksibendis* then later with the *Qadiris.* Both are made up of radical Islamic *Shari'a* believers. Over time my own belief in Islam and in the group got stronger. And I disliked the Jews and Christians. I pitied them for accepting a human being as their Lord and Savior. One day I thought I should get a Holy Bible and do some research to be able to criticize the Christian belief. I read a couple of pages from the Holy Bible and fell asleep. I dreamed that I was in a graveyard. All around me it was dark. The sun began to dawn, but where I was it was still dark. I tried to go to where the light was but was not successful. I woke up and was very disturbed. At the time I thought, *Why was I in the dark even though I tried very hard to reach the light? Why couldn't I do so?* (After I became a Christian I realized that it meant that I was spiritually dead. I didn't know anything about spiritual death at that time.)

> *Why was I in the dark even though I tried very hard to reach the light? Why couldn't I do so?*

At the age of 26, I was working with a couple of other people to translate some Islamic books that came from Saudi Arabia into Turkish. So we went to Arabia to meet with the group who supported us. While I was there I visited the grave of Muhammad at Mecca, the place of Islamic pilgrimage. To my surprise I felt nothing. I had expected to feel some spiritual peace, but I was not affected at all.

I met Isil, the woman who was to become my wife, at my cousin's house where I used to teach Islamic lessons to a group. She happened to be there on a visit to Turkey from England where she was raised and still lived. She too was a Muslim. I went to England to see her, and while I was in England, I also planned to see a Pakistani sheik with whom our group was in contact. But as soon as I got there I found out that he had died. This and many other things related to the translation were getting to be frustrating to me. I was trying to serve Allah, but it was like things were falling apart.

Isil, then my fiancé, and I decided to return to Turkey. Early in the morning I got up to get our plane tickets. The agency was still closed, so I decided to walk around a bit and wait till it opened. On my right I saw a cathedral. The doors were open and I found myself walking in. Anxiously, I sat there watching the people praying in silence. It was like I was glued to my seat. I looked around and thought, *What is this peace I feel?* I sat there for two hours even though I was uncomfortable with the fact I was experiencing peace in a cathedral.

We went back to Turkey and Isil and I got married and were living in Istanbul. She now joined the cult that I was leading. I had been in the group since I was a child. I had become very radical about my beliefs. The group was radical too, so they decided I would be a perfect leader. I also continued to translate the Islamic books.

MY WIFE HAS A VISION

One night, Isil told me that she saw a vision of Jesus and when she saw Him she felt power go right through her body. He had long hair and was dressed in white with a purple cloak. His heart was visible on His chest the way a broach would be. She said she just knew immediately in her heart that it was Jesus, though she didn't know how she knew.

> *One night, Isil told me that she saw a vision of Jesus and when she saw Him she felt power go right through her body.*

After that vision, she asked me if I would take her to a church. It was certainly a strange request. After all, I was a very zealous Islamic teacher. But we were just newlyweds, so I could not refuse her at that time. I took her to a church that visitors to Turkey go to see, Saint Antuan (St. Anthony) Roman Catholic Church in the Taksim Square area. I walked around inside the church as my wife sat praying in silence. This disturbed me very much. I was an Islamic leader and here we were in a church and my wife was praying! What on earth was happening? After that day we said nothing to each other about it and I pretended as if nothing had happened.

Six months later it was Ramadan. By this time I felt that our lives had become a disaster and every day it was getting worse. The project I was working on was getting to be a stressful chore. Eventually I became very frustrated and angry. One night I found myself furiously throwing books all over the room while screaming at Allah, "I have been serving you for years. I am trying to help other Muslims, but what are you doing? It's as if you are trying to stop me!" Isil was trying to calm me down at the same time she was picking up the books from the floor.

LIGHT, POWER, AND TRUTH

I left her in the room and went to the bedroom to calm down. I was very upset. I lay down, closed my eyes, and took a few deep breaths. All of a sudden I saw a bright light, and then there was a man standing in front of me. I could not really see His face, but I knew He was Jesus. The light around His head was very bright so I could not see His features, but, like my wife, in my heart I knew it was Jesus. I was not afraid but I was very astonished. He was standing very close to me. He started talking to me and asked me, "What are you looking for?"

I replied, "The truth."

Then He said, "I am the Way, the Truth, and the Life."

Then He came even closer to me and He put His hand on the top of my head. All of a sudden I felt an energy coming out of His hand going straight through my body. My whole body started to shake under the power coming from Him. I heard Isil coming in the room. She saw me shaking so badly and, since I had been so angry before, she thought I was having a nervous fit. She was calling out my name and crying, "What's the matter? What's happening?"

Jesus told me not to be afraid and also told me, "Tell your wife not to be afraid."

The shaking stopped and I told Isil not to be afraid and that I was seeing Jesus and we were talking to each other. She replied with shock, "If you are talking to Jesus, then ask Him if He heard me when I prayed at the church, and ask Him what I prayed about."

Before I could even ask Him, He replied, "I heard."

He started telling me about her prayer. I told her all that He told me. I was still seeing Jesus in the vision, but I heard her crying and she said,

"You really are talking to Him because I never told you what I prayed about." Then she said, "Ask Him what we should do."

I did and He said, "Repent and I will show you the way." Then He was gone.

I opened my eyes. I can't really explain how I felt at that moment because everything was such a shock to me. I looked at my wife. She was on her knees crying. I was crying also. We just did what He said and repented from our sins. I held my wife's hands and we repented together. We said, "We believe in You, Jesus. Thank You for coming into our lives."

> *We just did what He said and repented from our sins. I held my wife's hands and we repented together. We said, "We believe in You, Jesus. Thank You for coming into our lives."*

The next day we decided to go to the city of Taksim to buy a Bible. We got delayed quite a bit on the way, so before we got there we had little hope about the bookstore being open because it was rather late. To our surprise we found the bookstore open as if it was waiting for us to arrive. We got talking to the bookseller and he later told us, "I don't usually keep the shop open at this time but today I knew in my heart that something would happen. Now I know why the Lord wanted me to wait."

He was such a good man and we wound up learning a lot from him. He introduced us to his family and we became very close to them. He also took us to church every week. Of course we were very hungry to learn, and with his help we found out that there was a Bible school in another city. This led to Isil and I going to Bible school for two and a half years. That time was the best days of our lives. We fell in love with the Lord even more.

SAVED FROM DEATH

I had stopped teaching Islam after I became a Christian. At that time I was working on an Islamic encyclopedia so my excuse for not being with my Islamic group was that I had no time. Of course at that time I kept my belief in Jesus a secret because it would be very dangerous for me and my family if my radical Islamic group found out I believed in Jesus. Three months later we went to Bible school. We learned from a friend that a week after we left Istanbul to go to Bible school, the group that I had been in since I was a child had come looking for my wife and me to murder us because they had found out that we had became Christians. But the good Lord had saved us by sending us away from Istanbul just in time. Jesus has done and is continuing to do what He promised us. He is showing us the way!

> We learned from a friend that a week after we left Istanbul to go to Bible school, the group that I had been in since I was a child had come looking for my wife and me to murder us because they had found out that we had became Christians.

We have been serving the Lord for 11 years now, and our two daughters became Christians also and are serving Him. He is a good Teacher. He has taught us a lot through these years. It has not been very easy, but we have got through the hard times just by looking to Him and trusting in Him. He taught us how to resist the devil's games and how to survive through the stormy times of our lives. He taught us to be a family and how to be healed from our wounds. He has always been faithful. Thank You, Jesus, my Lord and Savior. You are surely the Truth, the Life, and the Way!

COMMENTARY BY FAISAL MALICK

One thing I have noticed about Muslims is they are always hungry to know the truth. Growing up as a Muslim myself, I have always had this same longing to know and understand the truth regardless of the cost. As you read these stories your heart may be drawn to Jesus and you may be thinking about the cost if you accept Jesus. You may be worried about your spouse or what may happen to your family. You have to take one step at a time and allow Jesus to guide your every step. Once you entrust your life into the hand of Jesus, He will guide you and show you the way.

> *Once you entrust your life into the hand of Jesus, He will guide you and show you the way.*

Take courage from the story of Isil. After her vision of Jesus she gave her heart to Him, but she did not try to convert her husband who was a leader of a fanatical Islamic cult. She kept walking with God and praying for her husband. She continued to honor and love her husband. Even when her husband was frustrated with Allah and throwing all his Islamic books on the floor, she went and picked them up and tried to comfort him.

On that day her husband, Cemil, reached the highest point of frustration in his life and cried out to God, desperate to know the truth. This is where Jesus intervened in his life and revealed Himself to Cemil—in the midst of his pain. In Cemil's encounter, Jesus even revealed the prayer that his wife prayed at the church, confirming to them that God hears and answers prayer. He cares for our every concern. This couple then began the journey of walking with God together. God connected them to the right family and provided them Bibles so they could grow in their relationships with God. He even preserved their lives from death and attacks. You do not have to be afraid because God will be with you always and protect you.

Islam and its culture often leave very little room for women and their rights, but Jesus demonstrates love for women and challenges men to love their wives like He loved the Church (the universal Body of Christ) and gave His life for it. Women also are challenged to respect and honor their husbands as they would honor the Lord. This cycle of love and honor is a picture of the relationship Jesus has with His Church. Christianity is about a real relationship with your Creator. True intimacy is the result of genuine relationships in life built on the Jesus kind of love. Once Jesus comes into your heart, your relationships will also change for the better as you change and become more like Jesus.

Real truth is much deeper than some ideology, fact, or idea. Truth is God Himself—eternal and unshakable, revealed in the person of Jesus. Truth is also light that has no shadow of variance or darkness in it. Truth does not change, but if you encounter the truth, your life will change. Jesus who is the Truth describes Himself this way:

> *I am Alpha and Omega, the beginning and the end, the first and the last* (Revelation 22:13 KJV).

Only one who is Truth can make such an eternal declaration. When you call out to God desiring to know truth sincerely from your heart, He will reveal Jesus to you. This is what happened to Isil and Cemil, a wonderful Muslim couple who both came to the knowledge of truth in Jesus Christ. They experienced the tangible power of His Presence. When you encounter the power of Almighty God, you will be changed forever. Jesus is the only way to freedom from lies and deception, and to salvation and eternal life. Remember the words of Jesus to Cemil and to others in this book also:

> ...*I am the way, the truth, and the life...* (John 14:6).

Are you looking for the truth? Then it is time for you to call out to God and ask Him sincerely to reveal the Truth to you.

God hears your heart and knows your thoughts. He has numbered every hair on your head and cares for you and loves you. He will answer the questions of your heart.

CHAPTER 8
I WENT TO HEAVEN
Jaafar Attaran

I WAS BORN IN A Muslim (Shiite) family in the south of Iran. All my relatives are believers in Islam and the teachings of Muhammad, Islam's prophet. I grew up with the same belief as my family, and I always thought that I was walking in the right and perfect way. My Islamic teachings taught me that the only way to satisfy God was to perfectly follow the Islamic *Shari'a* law. Since my parents adhered to strict Islamic tradition, I was three years old when they sent me to a *Madrasah*, which was a clergy house with some 50 to 100 other children where we were taught to memorize the Qur'an and *Shari'a* law. I would daily recite: "*Allah Akbar. La ilaha illa Allah, Muhammad rasul Allah.*" ("God is great. There is no other god but Allah and Muhammed is Allah's messenger.")

I came to America from Iran for further education at the age of 27. Though I had been raised a Shiite, I began attending a Sunni mosque because it was the only mosque in the city I was living in. It didn't matter to me. I just wanted to worship Allah. It was, however, not a good experience. Most of the mosque attendees were Sunnis from different parts of the Middle East and other parts of Asia. Since I was the only Shiite Muslim, it did not dawn on me that it would make a difference to them to see me among them. When the *muezzin* chanted the prayer calls five times a day,

Muslims lined up in rows where they bowed toward Mecca in prayer, so I naturally stood in line with them. Then the *imam*, the head of the mosque, lead the congregational prayer.

PERSECUTION AMONG MUSLIMS

I noticed I was gradually being elbowed out because of my body language. Shiites hold their hands with their palms together in front of their face when they pray, while Sunnis cross their arms against their chests. Sunni and Shiites believe in the same prophet Muhammad, but they have differences in the rituals pertaining to prayer. While this may seem insignificant, the other Muslims continued to treat me with disrespect. I couldn't understand why it should be such a conflict. Aren't all Muslims worshiping the same Allah? Finally, I left the mosque with a bitter feeling and never went back again.

> *Sunni and Shiites believe in the same prophet Muhammad, but they have differences in the rituals pertaining to prayer. I couldn't understand why it should be such a conflict. Aren't all Muslims worshiping the same Allah?*

I was a devoted Muslim for 31 years and considered myself a good Muslim. I practiced my daily prayers religiously, worshiped five times a day, fasted during Ramadan, and fulfilled all of the prescribed duties a good Muslim should complete, though I did so without reflecting on the meaning of the words. I just repeated them dutifully. I was taught that those who are killed in a jihad, a holy war against unbelievers, go directly to Heaven, but all others are put aside until judgment day when God will weigh their actions in life to see if they have done more good than bad. Also, I believed that Islam's prophet, Muhammad, was the last and greatest prophet who brought true religion to man. I studied the Qur'an to follow the Islamic religion as taught by the prophet Muhammad, which also included belief in other prophets of Islam: Noah, Abraham, Moses, and Jesus.

Two years after I left Iran for the United States for my further education, the Iranian Revolution began in 1979. The Shah of Iran left the country, and the Ayatollah Khomeini returned to Iran from exile in France. Even though I was living in the United States, it was very difficult for me at that time because my family was still living in Iran. The Islamic Revolution brought a great deal of bloodshed and pain to my homeland. About a year and a half later, the war between Iran and Iraq began, in 1980. Two of my 16-year-old cousins were killed, and two of my brothers got shot and were badly wounded while defending the southern borders of Iran against Iraqi forces. My family was displaced while trying to get away from scud missile attacks by Saddam Hussein into my hometown. The war went on for eight years, and the mental and emotional anguish contributed to the death of both my father and grandfather.

All this put much pressure on my mind and grieved me deeply. I asked God many times why two Muslim nations would have to fight each other. In my mind I was thinking Muslims should not be shedding the blood of other Muslims, but only the blood of unbelievers in Islam!

I FOUND A BOOK

It was about 1981 when I encountered many problems and I could not find any peace or solution for my difficulties. I had no trusted friends to go to, so I thought to turn to God for answers. One Sunday night in 1981, about 9:00 p.m., I was on my way home from the university I was attending. I stopped at a traffic light and noticed that a book was lying in the middle of the road. I opened the door and picked up the book and saw that it was a Bible. I didn't read it but put it away. After a few days, I grew curious to see what the difference is between the Qur'an and the Bible. So I took out the Bible I had found. I began to read the Qur'an in the morning and the Bible at night. In a short time I began to see some similarity between the Qur'an and the Bible, and some contradictions too!

When I began to read the Bible as a history book, I began to understand God better. He loved humanity. He created us! I knew about respect and honor, but love the way Jesus said to love seems to be missing in Islamic culture. The *Shari'a* laws tell Muslims if anyone leaves the religion of Islam and converts to another religion, such as Christianity or Judaism, not only is that person betraying his or her family, but also he or she is disgracing Islam. Muslims who convert are infidels and it is a duty of any Muslim to kill them and shed their blood. This would be honored by Allah, and the one who shed blood would gain his way to Heaven for the killing. As I was daily reading more of the Bible, I saw more consistency and authenticity of love and mercy in the Bible than in the Qur'an.

For 30 years of my life I had memorized the Qur'an. But it never gave me any inner peace. I also did not have a clear understanding of it because the Qur'an was written in the Arabic language and not in my own Iranian language of Farsi. Also, it does not follow clear paths of the stories like the Bible does. It never gave me any assurance of Heaven or of salvation for my soul. The Qur'an only tells its followers to do good works and follow the five pillars of Islam and leave the results to God!

The hostage crisis (where 52 Americans were held hostage by the Iranian government for 444 days), which had begun in Iran in 1979, by now was intensified, and I was in total despair. I felt so lonely and depressed that I cried out, "Help me, God! I'm at the end of my rope. I'm desperate, and I don't know which way to turn." I went into my bedroom and closed the door. I picked up the Bible that I had found in the street. I began to read it for myself. One day while reading the Bible, I cried out to God to reveal the truth to me.

"Which one of the great prophets that Islam has reverence for should I follow: Noah, Abraham, Moses, Jesus, or Muhammad? I must hear it from Your own mouth." I went on to pray, "If You are God, I want to know the truth. If it's Jesus, then show me Jesus, and if it's Muhammad, then show me Muhammad." After I spoke these words, I closed the Bible and set it on my nightstand and fell asleep.

"If You are God, I want to know the truth. If it's Jesus, then show me Jesus, and if it's Muhammad, then show me Muhammad."

THE DREAM OF HEAVEN

As I slept, I had a dream. In my dream I found myself in the ocean. The water was pulling me out farther into the deep. I was trying to swim to the shore, but there was now no sign of land. In the dream I was going up and down in the waves, underwater and then up above. I feared I was going to drown. There were heavy waves going from left and right, and I glanced to my side and saw giant rocks. I knew in my mind that if the waves threw me against those rocks I would be shattered into a million pieces. I cried out to God, "Help! Help! Help!" I kept going down in the water and coming up again.

Then I saw a hand coming out of the heavens, reaching down toward me. The hand pulled me out of the ocean and took me and placed me in His arms with His right arm around me. I felt heat coming from the side of His body to warm me up from the cold water. Then I looked at the hand and saw a nail scar on His palm.

At that moment I had a flash of memory from my childhood. I remembered a Greek Orthodox church in Iran with a crucifix. I thought, *Is this the same man who died on the Cross for His people?* I had heard a story about Him, but I never thought I'd see Him. I had this sudden memory while He had His arm around me. I looked up to see who this person was. He was dressed in a bright, white robe, and I saw a radiant aura that was so bright it kept me from seeing His face.

I said to Him, "Who are You?"

He said, "I am *Isa Massih*" (the Persian name for Jesus, the Messiah). "You called out to Me and I came to give you a new life. From now on you will be Mine and with Me forever."

I answered, still not at all sure about Him, "How do I know?"

He lifted His robe and showed me the nail scars on His feet. "Is that enough for you?" He asked.

I immediately felt a great peace. Then I knew this was Jesus who was crucified on the Cross, the One I had seen in the church building in Iran.

> Then I knew this was Jesus who was crucified on the Cross, the One I had seen in the church building in Iran.

Then He took my hand and we started walking on what seemed like a boardwalk. The shivering from the cold water immediately departed from me. As soon as I reached up with my eyes to see where we were, I saw the most spectacular place. It was a city that humankind could not possibly build, with handiwork that no human could possibly accomplish. It was all so very beautiful. Things were clear, like crystal glass, and gold. It was beyond anything I could possibly describe. We have nothing on earth such as this city. I experienced peace such as I had never known in my life and I felt entirely safe. I asked Him, "Where are we?" He looked at me and said, "Son, this is the new Jerusalem that My Heavenly Father built for Me. From this moment, you will be with Me always and I will take care of you."

I was so thrilled, like a little boy. I just wanted to know everything, touch everything. I turned around to look at Him and I was suddenly back in my bed. I wanted to go back to the dream, back to Jesus, back to Heaven. I felt afraid and I was weeping and sweating. I felt an anxiety that I could not understand, so I turned to my Bible. When I looked at it, I found it had been opened even though I had left it closed. It was opened to Matthew 6:25-26 (NIV):

> *Therefore I tell you, do not worry about your life, what you will eat or drink; or about your body, what you will wear. Is not life more important than food, and the body*

*more important than clothes? Look at the birds of the air; they do not sow or reap or store away in barns, and yet **your heavenly Father** feeds them. Are you not much more valuable than they?*

GOD IS OUR FATHER!

This went right into my spirit. We have a Father—God! *The God I am facing now,* I realized, *cares for me. He's not there to destroy me each time I commit sin. He loves me so much He came to me!* At that moment, I knew that the Man in my dream was the same Man whose representation was on the Cross in the church in Iran I saw as a child. Now I saw that relationship with God comes through Jesus! It was a turning point in my life. I realized that Jesus really did die on the Cross. He had died for my sin and released me from the death curse and the fear of going to hell. After that night, I decided to go to church and give my life to Jesus Christ. I felt such a relief, such a joy and peace, such a freedom from bondage that no man on this earth can give or fulfill.

> After that night, I decided to go to church and give my life to Jesus Christ. I felt such a relief, such a joy and peace, such a freedom from bondage that no man on this earth can give or fulfill.

Following a more complete study of the Bible, I became convinced that my salvation could be attained only through Jesus. The famous Scripture verse of John 3:16 says, *"For God so loved the world that He gave His only begotten Son, that whoever believes in Him should not perish but have everlasting life."* This emphasizes the wonderful truth about God's love for us. God came to earth in the form of a person. God created the world by His Word and His Spirit, so He could easily create a baby in Mary's womb by His Spirit. God does have a Son!

ASSURED OF HEAVEN

I read in the Bible that Jesus' disciples saw Him alive after He died and was raised from the dead, and they witnessed Him being taken into Heaven. When this reality touched my heart I realized fully that through Jesus Heaven is accessible to all who accept the truth of what He did. What's more, He had taken me there to show it to me! The Qur'an clearly teaches that each person will be judged for his or her actions on earth, and will be rewarded or punished in the afterlife according to his or her deeds:

> Every soul shall have a taste of death: and only on the Day of Judgment shall you be paid your full recompense. Only he who is saved from the fire (of hell) and is admitted to the garden (Heaven) will have attained the object (of life), for the life of this world is but goods and chattels of deception (Surah 3:185).

According to Islam we can never know until after we die if our good deeds outweigh our bad deeds.

But with Jesus, Heaven is assured to you not because of what you have done, but what He has done by dying on the Cross for the sins of human-kind. The only work that is required of us is to believe (have faith in) this truth, that God came as a Man and took the responsibility for sin Himself in order for man to gain access to His presence in Heaven. No one could be good enough to earn acceptance into God's holy Presence, except the Holy One Himself—Jesus.

> *But God, being rich in mercy, because of His great love with which He loved us, even when we were dead in our transgressions* [sins], *made us alive together with Christ (by grace you have been saved), and raised us up with Him, and seated us with Him in the heavenly places in Christ Jesus, so that in the ages to come He might show the surpassing riches of His grace in kindness toward us in Christ Jesus. **For by grace you have been saved** through*

faith; and that not of yourselves, it is **the gift of God; not
as a result of works**, so that no one may boast (Ephesians
2:4-9 NASB).

Jesus said, *"Do not let your hearts be troubled. Trust in God; trust also in
Me"* (John 14:1 NIV). When I read these passages, the dream and Heaven
became even more of a reality. I felt overjoyed and had such great peace,
knowing I could trust Jesus with my eternal destiny.

MUHAMMAD IS STILL DEAD, BUT WHERE'S JESUS?

*I know that the prophet Muhammad is buried in Medina, Saudi Ara-
bia, but I saw the empty tomb of Jesus in Jerusalem with my own
eyes. It is where Jesus' body was buried, but it is empty!*

Once I would not have thought to travel to Israel, but after these events
I wanted to see it. I traveled to Israel in 1987. I know that the prophet
Muhammad is buried in Medina, Saudi Arabia, but I saw the empty tomb
of Jesus in Jerusalem with my own eyes. It is where Jesus' body was buried,
but it is empty! The Bible tells of how the disciples put Him in the tomb
but then He was no longer there. Two angels reported to them saying, "He
has risen"! (See Matthew 27:57-60; 28:5-7.) I know when I die I will be
with the same Jesus whom I saw in my dream.

I was baptized at the baptismal site where John baptized people in the
Jordan River on October 7, 1987, in Israel. Once I was a lost sinner, but
now I am found and saved. I no longer live in the darkness, but He made
me to be a light in the darkness.

I pray that all people in Iran and around the world receive the same
forgiveness and peace that I received through Jesus Christ. I pray for that
day when God will fully bless the Muslim people with the salvation only
Jesus can bring. Glory is to our God, the Father of our Lord Jesus Christ.

COMMENTARY BY FAISAL MALICK

The war between Iran and Iraq in 1980 put tremendous pressure on Jaafar. Two Muslim nations fighting with one another, the death of family members, the bloodshed of siblings, and the resulting death of his father and grandfather left him desperate for answers. So he cried out to God for help. In response to his prayer he found a mysterious book in the middle of an intersection—a Bible. He began to read it, and as he did, 30-plus years of beliefs and faithfulness to Islam were challenged. Initially, Jaafar began to read the Bible as a history book and not entirely for spiritual reasons, but as he read, he was challenged with answers to questions that Islam did not have. This left him perplexed with many more questions to reconcile. But all his questions were settled with a supernatural peace when he encountered Jesus in a dream.

We live in a world filled with constant conflict and confusion that often promises peace but cannot deliver. Meanwhile, even in the midst of turmoil and tribulation, Jesus promises to give peace that extends beyond the scope of our understanding.

Let's read this powerful statement Jesus makes in the midst of a conversation about the Father with His disciples.

> *Peace I leave with you, My peace I give to you; not as the world gives do I give to you. Let not your heart be troubled, neither let it be afraid* (John 14:27).

Jesus promises to give peace that extends beyond the scope of our understanding.

Let me give you some context for this statement. Jesus has just finished telling them:

> *...No one comes to the Father except through Me* (John 14:6).

In this same conversation He has just shared with them:

> *...He who has seen Me has seen the Father...* (John 14:9).

What is this peace that only Jesus can give? This peace that Jesus is referring to is a relationship with God—a revelation of the Father. Jesus is the only Way to the Father and the only One who can reveal the Father. The realization that Jesus came from the Father is the beginning of peace. When you realize who Jesus is, you will experience the peace that comes from God. When you experience Jesus you experience the Father. When you see Jesus you see the Father, and the peace that is the abode of Heaven becomes your dwelling place on earth. This is why Jesus said, *"...Let not your heart be troubled, neither let it be afraid"* (John 14:27).

Let's look at another verse where Jesus mentions this peace.

> *These things I have spoken to you, that in Me you may have peace. In the world you will have tribulation; but be of good cheer, I have overcome the world* (John 16:33).

As long as you live in this world you will experience trouble, but in Jesus alone you experience the peace of God.

Notice the first part of the statement Jesus made: *"These things I have spoken to you that in Me you may have peace...."* What were the things that Jesus spoke that cause us to have peace in Him? Let's see:

> *For the Father Himself loves you, because you have loved Me, and have believed that I came forth from God. I came forth from the Father and have come into the world. Again, I leave the world and go to the Father* (John 16:27-28).

He is talking about a relationship with God that you can have once you believe and recognize Jesus is the Living Word that came from the Father, died on the Cross, rose again from the dead, and returned to the Father. This is the beginning of an authentic relationship with God. A relationship where your prayers will be heard and you will hear the voice of the Almighty. A relationship where you will find true forgiveness for your sin and know peace in the holy Presence of God rather than mere empty rituals and regulations. I know you may have many questions, but when you entrust your life to Jesus and surrender your heart to Him, then the Holy Spirit will come and abide in you and you will understand what Jesus meant when He said:

> *At that day you will know that I am in My Father, and you in Me, and I in you* (John 14:20).

Think and ponder the above statement and imagine what Jesus is promising you. Remember what Jesus said, *"...in Me you may have peace...."*

> When you entrust your life to Jesus and surrender your heart to Him, then the Holy Spirit will come and abide in you and you will understand what Jesus meant.

Regardless of the storms in your life—external or internal—if you trust in Jesus and surrender your heart to Him, like Jaafar, you too can experience the peace that comes from Jesus and know the Father.

You do not have to wait till you die without any guarantee of salvation, hoping for mercy on the day of judgment. You can trust in Jesus today and secure God's mercy and salvation and experience eternal life from this moment forward.

If you are ready to know this peace, then put your faith in Jesus and pray this prayer with me.

> *Father in Heaven, I thank You for putting this book in my hands and that You are revealing things about Yourself I didn't know before. Open up my understanding to know the depth of Your love. Jesus, I want to know the peace that only You can give. I surrender my heart and life to You and I believe You came from the Father to earth and died on the Cross for me and rose again from the dead. I ask You to come into my heart and give me eternal life that I may*

know You are in the Father and I in You even as You are in me.

Let me also pray for you.

Father, I pray that You open the eyes of this person's heart and reveal Jesus to him or her.

CHAPTER 9

MY HEART THIRSTS FOR ALMIGHTY GOD
Mohammad Seyedzadeh

I WAS IN MY TEENS when the Revolution happened in my country of Iran. With all that was taking place, I developed a fascination for more of Islam than I already knew. I had been brought up in the mosque. My mother was a devoted Muslim, though my father was more liberal. We supported our faith and mosque financially even when we didn't have enough money for our life essentials. I fell in love with Islam and I devoted my life to it. I read whatever I could and eventually had some 3,200 books in my library at home. Most of them were Islamic books. I became passionate about my decision to become an orthodox Muslim. I won the second prize in Islamic *Ahkam* (laws) and, among friends, I was considered the best source to ask and check for questions in regard to Islamic *Ahkam*.

I continued over the years to follow Islam with all my heart, memorizing the Qur'an, with the intent of being a true Muslim. In my route to work I used to pass by a church. At the stop in front of the church I would whisper in prayer, "Allah, one day I'm going to destroy these places for you." The church for me (as for many Muslims) was a symbol of worshiping God incorrectly and believing in polytheism (we thought the Christians worshiped three gods). I couldn't understand how the

Christians could ignore the supremacy of Islam and the fact that Islam is the only way of being a true servant of God.

> *I couldn't understand how the Christians could ignore the supremacy of Islam.*

LONGING TO BE CLOSER TO GOD

I had beautiful, devoted Muslim friends who were sincere and humble. Living exemplary lives as Muslims was our passion every day of our lives, and we pushed ourselves to the limit. Islam teaches that a person can get a promotion for praying the lengthy night prayers, which should be prayed hidden behind closed doors after midnight. This prayer time is not like daytime prayers. If a Muslim misses the day prayers, he must do them later. Doing the night prayers is encouraged *(mostahab)*, but only a handful of believers choose to consider them a *must* in order to get closer to God. It requires more than discipline; it requires a passion to sacrifice your sound sleep every night in order to seek a way to get closer to your creator! I even used to push to catch up with the ones I missed *(ghaza)*. That was my passion for my maker!

I always did these lengthy prayers sincerely and with proper pronunciation (which is important for Muslims) just to get a bit closer to him. My faith taught me that no human is worthy to be allowed to get close to God's holy presence. Perfect God (Allah) was unable to communicate with imperfect man directly without harming him, regardless of imperfect man's love and passion for him. Repeating the same verses and sentences was allowed only in one language—Arabic. Yet maintaining a monologue in which the servant talks in hope of being heard by Allah was not enough for me.

> Perfect God (Allah) was unable to communicate with imperfect man directly without harming him, regardless of imperfect man's love and passion for him.

I was very much respected because of my sincerity and knowledge in Islam, but position and indulging in people's attention wasn't what I was after. I began to realize that the mountaintop I was standing on wasn't high enough for my passion to get closer to God. So, since education is very much promoted in Islam, I decided instead of standing still at that dead-end street, I would put my passion into education and grow more in other aspects of my existence. I decided to drop the garment of fundamentalism and continue the path of life through further education and learning. Since universities and available fields were limited back home, I decided to go to abroad. I spoke about this with my English teacher. I told her that my reading and writing was good but I had difficulty listening and following English conversations. She told me of a church where the preaching was in English and suggested it would be a very good place to work on my listening skills. So I began going to that church, a Catholic church for English speakers in Tehran. I went for a few weeks and to me it was just another holy place that belonged to a religion in error.

I WENT TO SAVE MY FRIEND FROM CHURCH

My English teacher and I talked occasionally about churches and she was like a caring mother to me. One day she told me of a friend she sent to a different church which preached in both Farsi and English. She was disappointed because the Muslim friend she sent to that church converted to Christianity. Surprised at such a silly change, I said, "They don't know their Islamic faith enough or they wouldn't convert." So my English teacher and I decided to go to this church and then pick up her friend from there and go for a coffee and straighten her out.

We arrived there after the sermon was over and people were praying. The moment I entered I felt different. I felt a peaceful presence that I never had felt with that intensity in any of the holy places I had been to before. It was a very simple building with no pictures or sculpture, yet the presence of God was so noticeable, it made me sit in respect. I bowed my head as many others did in prayer.

A man I didn't know came up to me and began to talk to me, asking how I was. Then he started talking about God's love and how he was saved from sin as well as from heroin addiction and now he was serving God in his church. This was all new and fascinating to me. While he was talking of God's love and how He seeks to save sinners, I remembered verses in the Qur'an that say that Allah ambushes the sinner. This concept that God loves the sinners and wants to save them was strange to me. The man invited me to come back again. A few years previously, I had read the Gospel of John and a few books about Christianity according to Muslims that showed the flaws in Christianity as well as how to debate skillfully with Christians. Reading the Gospel of John didn't fascinate me at all back then. Now I decided to investigate the faith further and so I kept going back to the church for weeks.

> This concept that God loves the sinners and wants to save them was strange to me.

I met different people who told me how they were saved by the love of Christ from different addictions and from a sinful lifestyle. For a devoted Muslim, such as me, avoiding a sinful lifestyle meant hard work, discipline, and fighting the evil inside of me as well as evil outside. These people were talking about a rapid transformation that was happening in a different way. A very different way!

JESUS APPEARS TO MY FRIEND

One fellow, who a few years later became my best friend, told me how he ended up coming to Christ. He told me he was planning to end his life when he was completely discouraged and hopeless. Just before he was about to commit suicide, all of a sudden Jesus appeared to him in his room although he had no background in Christianity at all. Jesus told him, "Go to a church." While he was telling me his story, I couldn't help laughing at him in my heart. I thought he was delusional or something, saying that Jesus came and spoke to him.

> *I sang along to the hymns but not the blasphemous parts such as "Jesus is Lord" or "Son of God." I would never, and could never, repeat those words.*

I continued to go to the church for about three months, trying not to miss any meetings and listening carefully. I still considered myself a Muslim and considered Christians in that church to be people who loved God but were in error. I sang along to the hymns but not the blasphemous parts such as "Jesus is Lord" or "Son of God." I would never, and could never, repeat those words.

A DREAM I COULD NOT FORGET

One day I was lying down on the couch reading a book, and as often happened, I fell asleep while reading. I suddenly saw myself in a dream-like state exactly where I was in my room. I saw my room was full of smog and I was right in the middle of that toxic smog (spiritually speaking). At the door I saw the presence of a Man. I immediately knew it was Jesus despite the fact I couldn't see His appearance. Sometimes when I share this with people they ask me, "How did you know He was Jesus? Was He like pictures in some churches? Did He introduce Himself?"

I always answer, "My friend, when you see Him, you cannot mistake Him for anyone else. The spirit world has its own reality and is not dependent upon natural appearance."

> *When you see Him, you cannot mistake Him for anyone else. The spirit world has its own reality and is not dependent upon natural appearance.*

While He was looking at me through the smog, and without hearing His verbal voice, I "heard" Him telling me: "This is your last chance. Are you coming after Me or should I leave?" I immediately snapped out of that dream and I sat up. For a moment I was going to laugh exactly as I laughed at my friend who told me his story a few weeks earlier about Jesus coming to him and telling him to go to church. But a voice from inside asked me, "Could you laugh at what you witnessed personally?" I was touched, but decided not to share this with anyone for a while.

The next day nothing miraculous happened and life went on as usual. Even though I knew I did not reject Him, I still didn't consider myself a follower of Jesus. But the next time I went to church I noticed a difference. It seemed I could understand the depth of the words being communicated. I was reading the same Bible I had read before and heard before, but now the meanings behind what Jesus was teaching were being revealed to me. It was like my eyes and ears were closed before and were now opened. I understood far more than I ever did before.

The next month or two were very hard for me. Following each sermon, the leaders asked if anyone wanted to come forward to accept the Lord. It was such a difficult thing to me. I could hear the call that was drawing me forward and I wanted to be embraced by Jesus, whom I got to know recently. But I wrestled with thinking, *What if someone knows me?* There is a law in Iran called the Apostasy Law. Conversion from Islam to another religion is punishable by death. All types of thoughts made me hesitate, despite the fact that Jesus and His teachings were touching my heart.

MY WORLD CHANGES

The knowledge of the love of God was taking root inside me each time I heard His words or the story of a lost individual who was saved from their sinful life by Him. One day I just found myself unable to resist and I went forward. I kneeled down and prayed like I was just talking in my own language with Him. I said to Him, "I love You and I want the honor of You ruling my heart." It was as simple as that. I don't know if it was couple of minutes or half an hour—time becomes irrelevant in His Presence! But when I stood up I could swear I was in a different world. Everything was different to me. It was like walking on the clouds. I felt a complete transformation in my mind and heart. This person who had been so involved in being the perfect Muslim, who had studied so much of Islam, had now entered in a loving relationship with God through Jesus Christ!

> *Prayer was not something the body had to endure by the command of the mind. Prayer was entering His real Presence, a dialogue with Him, and not just a "one man talking with no response" experience.*

From then on, my prayers were not memorized verses or sentences, they were conversations with God. Can you imagine how I felt? Prayer was not something the body had to endure by the command of the mind. Prayer was entering His real Presence, a dialogue with Him, and not just a "one man talking with no response" experience. My body and soul and heart were continually anxious to get into His divine Presence.

The night before my baptism I was in prayer and the Lord took me on a journey from the beginning of my life. He showed me all the events and moments when I had been in different accidents and was about to die but He protected me. He wanted me to live, as He had plans for my life. All the events of my life made sense then and didn't seem so random anymore. In the past, if anyone in my family had converted and wanted to be baptized, I would have been the first person to persecute and even kill them, and I would have considered it obedience to God.

> *In the past, if anyone in my family had converted and wanted to be baptized, I would have been the first person to persecute and even kill them, and I would have considered it obedience to God.*

THIRTY PEOPLE IN MY FAMILY ACCEPT JESUS

As it turned out, it proved to be much easier to share my faith than I thought it might be, as I had the advantage of being known as a good, devoted Muslim. Shortly after my baptism I found myself sharing with my mother, a devoted Muslim, about taking my younger nephew and nieces to church. I thought there would be no hope for the older ones. Very calmly and clearly, in what I now know was the Holy Spirit's leading speaking through her, my mother said, "Why don't you take your sister to church instead?"

I thought my sister would be the last person to be open to Jesus as she was never passionate about God by any means. But I felt it was what God wanted, so I invited her to meet me without telling her the reason. I took her to the church without saying anything and just told her, "Come in and listen and see what you think." So she came in and listened. I could see she was touched. This was a Friday night. I invited her to come again on Sunday. The second time she was touched even more, and after the sermon she asked me if many people in the church were Muslims. This was her respectful and indirect way of asking me if I had converted. I told her, "You are the only one." The third time she came she gave her heart to the Lord. It was dramatic and she became one of the most passionate evangelists I know.

Another brother who is much older than me was also a man who had had no place for God in his heart and life. But I saw Jesus transform him, as He did my sister, until they both became completely different people and the love of God was all they cared for after that. The brother and sister who surrendered their hearts to Jesus were the same ones I had no success in bringing close to God while I was a Muslim.

God had my sister and I speak among devoted Muslims, and in a matter of a year, close to 30 people just in my family alone came to the Lord! Each family member came in a unique way with his or her own experience with God. For example, my older brother's father-in-law was very stubborn. One day when everyone else was going to church, being sick with severe arthritis he stayed in bed. When my brother and the family came back home, they found him unable to talk for hours. Finally when he could speak again, he told them how Jesus had come into his room. He became a beautiful Christian that day and told the family, "When I die, be sure you bury me as a Christian, not a Muslim."

HEALINGS AND MIRACLES

Muslims believe in miracles, although they are very uncommon in our faith. Miracles and healings and miraculous life changes were everyday stories in our church. One fascinating miracle with which I was involved happened to a lady in the church who had terminal cancer. This was during the last years of the war between Iran and Iraq. Some church members with illnesses or the elderly and small children in the family who couldn't cope with the stress of missiles hitting the city would spend some time or weekends in a property in the suburbs which had a big garden. This place was also used for church gatherings and conferences. One night a group of us stood beside this woman's bed and prayed for her because her doctor said she would not live till morning. The next morning we came back to help with arrangements for her to be moved to a funeral home or whatever we needed to do for her. To our shock and surprise, she was out of the bed with a mop in her hand and she was cleaning the floors! She became a living testimony that Jesus heals to a lot of people.

> *Miracles and healings and miraculous life changes were everyday stories in our church.*

As for me at this time, I was in the end of my last year of university getting my Bachelor of Science degree. As a convert I couldn't go back to my work because it was a government job. To protect the non-Christian members of my family and to prevent them from being affected by the consequences that could come as a result of my conversion, which could mean even my death, I decided to leave Iran. Within a few years, almost all of the converted members in my family left except a few in other cities, most of whom live "underground" as Christians. There was a certain amount of persecution from those in my family who did not become Christians, but it was very insignificant in our case. When a person converts from Islam, it is considered rejection of the prophet Muhammad and is considered the worst thing one could do. Many believers face much harsher reactions from their families than I did even though their lifestyles were dramatically changed for the better!

I have many good memories of sharing my new faith with my Muslim brothers. Christians actually have some beliefs in common in Muslims. Muslims believe that God talked to Abraham, who was called God's friend, and they believe Moses talked to God. Christianity is a loving relationship between God and people. It is the voice of God talking to us through Jesus and saying God does not want us to suffer. He grieves over the injustice in our society. Most important of all, He wants to fill our hearts with His joy so that we no longer have to have the pain and sorrow that we experience in our hearts and souls when we don't know Him personally, when all we know of Him is His absence. He is not after our lengthy prayers or worship; He is after our hearts. He has no desire to force Himself or His rules on us by physical means, but He wants us to give ourselves a chance to know Him. We all want to find Him and hear from Him, but our hope vanishes when we struggle more and don't get anywhere.

> *We all want to find Him and hear from Him, but our hope vanishes when we struggle more and don't get anywhere.*

I want to say to you reading this: Talk to Him and open your heart for Him to talk to you. What is there to lose? You have only much to gain—a relationship with God as you've always wanted. Many have done just this and then told me of their awesome experiences. Jesus says, *"I knock at the door of your heart and if you open I will come in to you"* (see Rev. 3:20). We never have to wait to be worthy of His presence. He took care of that. He made us worthy when He died for our sins so that now we can come to God and be in His Presence. He says to you, "Come!"

COMMENTARY BY FAISAL MALICK

Mohammad's path was graced with many opportunities to hear about Jesus. Not everyone is so fortunate. He made fun of his friend who had a vision of Jesus and went to church. Maybe like Mohammad you are very intellectual or highly educated and mentally astute when it comes to the things of religion. In spite of his expertise and knowledge about Islam and its laws, his heart was still longing to know more of God. I believe you are sincere in your desire to learn more about God and you want to follow Him with all your heart.

Everyone has their own journey of how they come to realization of the truth in life. For some it happens suddenly, and for others it takes time and a series of divine moments along the way. One thing is for sure, it always starts with a heart seeking answers.

What is so interesting about Mohammad's story is that not only did he come to know the truth, but many Muslims in his family have come to recognize Jesus as Lord and Savior of their lives as well. The life they all experienced can be described like a river of living water that flows from the throne of God and the Lamb to the thirsty heart and soul (see Rev. 22:1).

Once you believe in Jesus, your life becomes a channel of this life-giving river. At one of the holy festivals of celebration, Jesus got the crowd's attention with a loud voice. Here's what happened:

> *On the last day, that great day of the feast, Jesus stood and cried out, saying, "If anyone thirsts, let him come to Me and drink. He who believes in Me, as the Scripture has said, out of his heart will flow rivers of living water"* (John 7:37-38).

Jesus is inviting those of us who are spiritually thirsty to come and believe on Him so He can quench our thirst with truth and our hearts will be like a river flowing from God.

When you come to know Jesus you become a brand-new creation—a species of origin that never existed before. You literally become a brand-new person with a new life. Your spirit man is reborn by the breath of God. Salvation is not just forgiveness of sin; it is also a complete change of identity and spiritual DNA. God imparts His own nature to you and places His own righteousness inside your heart. This is what it means to know Jesus.

> *God imparts His own nature to you and places His own righteousness inside your heart.*

Christianity is not a license to sin but the exchange of your old sinful nature for a brand-new nature through Jesus Christ. God's nature takes residence on the inside of you and a process of change begins in your life from the inside out. You cannot change yourself, but God can, by giving you a brand-new heart. Jesus wants to give you a brand-new heart and make your heart the temple of God on earth (see Ezek. 36:26). He wants to dwell in your heart through His Holy Spirit. He wants to be the supernatural well of Zamzam in your heart.

Four thousand years ago when our father Ishmael was in the wilderness dying of thirst, it was water from a well that saved his life (see Gen. 21:17). Ishmael means "God hears," and God was faithful to respond to the cry of Ishmael's heart while he was in the wilderness. God is also faithful to hear the cry of your heart to know truth and experience life. You may be spiritually thirsty for living water in what may seem like a desert-like place in your life. God desires to open your eyes and show you the well of living water, which is Jesus, so you can know the Father.

With a sincere heart and honest thirst for truth let your desire be made known to God. Let me take a moment to pray for you.

> *Father, I pray that You awaken the cry of this person's heart and satisfy his or her spiritual thirst for a relationship with You. Jesus, make this person's heart a supernatural well of Zamzam overflowing with life.*

CHAPTER 10

BURIED ALIVE AND LEFT FOR DEAD

Steven Masood

I WAS BORN IN THE village of Tarnab near Peshawar in the northwest frontier region of Pakistan. Tarnab is around 170 miles east of Kabul in Afghanistan. Like many Muslims, my parents considered that Islam covered the whole sphere of one's life: religious, social, and political. I was raised to believe the same. Like some other Muslim children, at about six or seven years old, I was sent to the mosque where I learned to read the Qur'an in Arabic, which was not my native language. At a later age Muslims may come to know the meaning of the Qur'an but not many children learn it with its translation. I was one of the fortunate ones. By the age of 13 I had memorized the entire Holy Qur'an, which was encouraged by Muhammad, the prophet of Islam, but is not something many Muslims do.

Islam is not one united religion. There are several sects and they are further divided into denominations and splinter groups. A few of these groups are not even accepted as Muslims by the mainline Muslims, the Sunni.

As a teenager, I was facing many problems. One of the major ones was that my family were *Ahmadi*, followers of a sect of Islam that other

Muslims do not accept, and so we were treated as non-Muslims. I used to wonder, *If we believe in the same creed and the same Qur'an, why do other people say we are not Muslims?* Little did I realize that this question would take me on a journey to embrace the truth at any cost.

> *If we believe in the same creed and the same Qur'an, why do other people say we are not Muslims?*

The founder of the *Ahmadiyya* sect, Mirza Ghulam Ahmad (1835-1908), claimed that he received a revelation from God to bring revival to Islam. Before his claim to be a reviver of Islam, he followed the orthodox Muslim ideas. After his initial foundation of the sect *Ahmadiyya*, he claimed that Jesus was crucified but revived and later died at the seashore of Galilee. Ten years later, Ghulam Ahmad wrote a book, *Masih Hindustan Main* ("Jesus in India"), in which he claimed that Jesus actually survived and was saved by a miraculous ointment. Jesus thereafter traveled to India where he died at the age of 120. Ghulam Ahmad asserted that he himself was the second coming of Jesus. It was in such a belief system that I grew up. Because we believed we had the truth that the Sunnis (the major sect of Islam) didn't know, I questioned why on earth God kept a secret for so many years only to reveal it through the *Ahmadiyya* sect in Islam in the nineteenth century almost 1,400 years after Muhammad. This caused me to compare Sunni orthodoxy with that of *Ahmadiyya*.

HOW I BECAME A SUNNI MUSLIM

At about the age of 18, I left my parents' home and became a Sunni Muslim. I wanted to know every major aspect of Islam. I met a Sunni Muslim family who were very influential people. They introduced me to some honorable Muslim scholars and I had many discussions with them. In spite of this I continued to have one major dilemma. Even if I followed Islam entirely, what would be my eternal destiny? This life is going to end, maybe tomorrow, maybe in a minute. How could I be sure of my life in the paradise of God? Muslims do believe in the hereafter and the judgment.

But what seemed so horrible to me is that even the most sincere Muslim would find that on his own he cannot save himself from the eternal fires of hell. Islam does not have a savior. Muslims believe that if we do good things we will go to paradise. But is it so? Is there an assurance? Islam does not present assurance. Even Muhammad, the prophet of Islam, himself was uncertain of his eternal fate at the end of his life. In fact the Qur'an states that God asked him to tell his followers, speaking about himself, "I am no new thing among the messengers, nor know I what will be done with me or with you..." (Surah 46:9).

MY FURTHER DISCOVERY INTO ISLAMIC BELIEFS

I learned that the whole of Muslim orthodoxy believes that Jesus, as a prophet, ascended into Heaven but did not die on the Cross. He was not even crucified. In contrast, the *Ahmadiyya* sect in which I was raised believes that Jesus was crucified but did not die on the Cross. What happened on the Cross then? How was He released from the Cross? When I studied all these things I wondered why Allah, who is omnipotent, would tell his prophet these contradictions.

When I was about the age of 13, I got a copy of the Gospel of John from a friend, who got it from someone who had been distributing Christian tracts in the Urdu language of my people. The first thing that came to my mind was, *Is this the Injil (the Gospel) that was revealed to Jesus?* As a Muslim, I was taught that God sent lots of books through the prophets—even the holy books, like the Torah, to Moses. He also gave the *Zabur* (the Psalms) to David, and the *Injil* was given to Jesus, but the Christians and Jews got together and corrupted the words and put their own words in the mouths of the prophets. So 600 years later God sent one more prophet, this time not from the Jews but from the Ishmaelites, to give the uncorrupted word. His name was Muhammad, and he lived from A.D. 571 to 632. I was also taught that God gave every scripture in Arabic to the prophets, and then the prophets interpreted their messages into the language of their people. So when I saw the

Gospel for the first time, my first thought was to ask why it was not in Arabic.

That night I began to read straight through it. I was surprised! It was different from what I expected. This was not the same Jesus I read about in the Qur'an. There are some 90 verses about Jesus in the Qur'an. They say that He is the Word of God and the Spirit of God, and yet He is just a prophet. The Qur'an also says that they (the Jews) did not kill Him or crucify Him. So according to the Qur'an, Jesus was not killed.

The next day I asked my Islamic studies teacher if God is our father. He came to know that I read it in the Gospel. He showed me his whole Bible with the four Gospels in the New Testament and told me: "We Muslims believe Jesus received one Gospel, but these Christians have four, and no one knows which one is true. Above all, don't you recite in your prayers—*Allah begetteth not, nor he is begotten. How can God have a son when he has no wife, no consort?*" He took the Gospel from me and I promised him not to study such things again.

> "We Muslims believe Jesus received one Gospel, but these Christians have four, and no one knows which one is true."

A Muslim recites chapter 112 of the Qur'an in Arabic during his prayers, which take place five times a day: "Say, God is one. He is aloof. He begetteth not, nor is he begotten. And there is none comparable to him." Imagine now with me a Muslim hearing or reading in the Bible, *"For God so loved the world that He gave His only begotten Son, that whoever believes in Him shall not perish but have everlasting life"* (John 3:16). A practicing Muslim's response would be, "Allah forbid, Allah forbid. That's not possible."

My teachers used to always tell me, "God cannot have a son when he has no wife and no consort." With such a thought I stopped my search from going further.

Two years later I was given a complete New Testament. I was 15 years old—and a rascal. I was of a poor family but had found several ways to support myself. Apart from menial jobs and errands for people, I did homework for other kids for money in order to bear the expenses of my education and other needs. Several times I was caught because of my handwriting. I told the other kids not to sit in one place. There were 65 to 70 children in a class. But if five or six of them sat in the same row and their papers had the same handwriting, the teacher would know.

Also, among the eight-hour classes, four of those hours were spent on Islamic studies. When my colleagues didn't do their homework, they asked me, "Would you please divert the attention to the teacher to something else?" I would do something wrong so I would be punished but they wouldn't be. I got money for doing those things in order to pay for my education because my parents couldn't afford my education.

During lectures my mind would wonder, questioning what was said by the teacher. I wanted to know how, when, and where? The teacher would say, "It is written." I wanted to know why. One day I was beaten for asking too many questions. The teachers said that Muhammad was inspired. I asked, "How did he know he was inspired?"

The teacher said, "The Qur'an says so."

> I wanted to know how, when, and where? The teacher would say, "It is written." I wanted to know why.

I asked, "But where does it say he was inspired and how was he inspired?" When I asked questions like this again, I was beaten again.

Muslims believe that through Muhammad, Allah completed his message. No new revelation was to be sent after him. In fact, Muhammad was the last prophet according to Islam. Here was my problem: Just before his death, Muhammad claimed that Allah told him: "Today we have completed your religion" (Surah 5:5). This is why Muslims believe no more revelation would be given after Muhammad and the Qur'an. So my question was, "How come this man, Ghulam Ahmad from India, the man who started my family's faith, came up with a new revelation?"

Also, Ghulam Ahmad denied what other Muslims believe about what Jesus would do at His second coming. Muslims are waiting for the coming of Jesus. According to Muslims of the Shia sect, when Jesus comes back He will be siding with the *Mahdi*, the twelfth imam, who will appear with Jesus or a few years before Him. The Sunni, the majority sect of Islam, believe in a different *Mahdi* who will come and take control. In spite of such a difference, the majority of Muslims believe that both Jesus and the *Mahdi* will wage war against infidels. Jesus will ask all Christians and Jews to become Muslims. *Dajjal*, the antichrist, will appear with his armies. He will be killed and his armies, including opposing Jews and Christians, will be destroyed. Islam will be established all over the world. Then Jesus will take a woman for a bride. Muslims believe every prophet was a male and married. Jesus was never married, so when He comes back, He will marry and have children and later die and be buried next to Muhammad. After a few years of all this, judgment day will take place.

> *I was impressed by the courage of the preacher who had given a copy of the New Testament to me. My father and his friends went and beat him almost to death, for giving the Scripture to a Muslim.*

At the age of 15 I was questioning all these things. I wondered, *What should I do?* I decided to go back to the Qur'anic teaching in order to be a good Muslim. I also read the New Testament. The more reading I did, the more the New Testament helped me to understand some things, but I believed the New Testament was corrupted. I just wanted to be a good Muslim, and to follow Muhammad to the letter. Personally, I was impressed by the courage of the preacher who had given a copy of the New Testament to me. My father and his friends went and beat him almost to death, for giving the Scripture to a Muslim—me. I admired this man's courage to be willing to die for his faith and to be obedient to the great commission to go and share the Gospel.

I WANTED TO BE A SCHOLAR OF ISLAMIC STUDIES

I left my home at age 18 to begin a search toward becoming a scholar in Islamic studies, and to help others be good Muslims. I would ask Allah and pray to him, "Show me your way." But then my heart would ask me, "Isn't Islam already the way?" I studied and had discussions with scholars. One thing I wanted to know was: How do I know Allah loves me? The Qur'an presents conditional love. It is I who has to take the first step to love Allah and then perhaps in return he would love me. I asked the various scholars, "Sir, how can I know I have loved this god enough so that now he is loving me?"

"It is not possible to know," they would answer.

Their conclusion of such a discussion was to tell me not to question Allah, the prophet, or the Qur'an. "Allah exists," they would say, "so don't even think about it. What he has revealed to Muhammad, don't question, just accept it. And don't question or doubt the integrity of the Qur'an." Still, I wanted to know how we could be sure we would achieve the goal of paradise. What I really wanted to know was how not to go to hell. The Qur'an talks about hell for those who do bad things, but says that if you do good things, perhaps Allah will accept you. Muslims believe Allah sent 124,000 prophets into this world to lead people into the straight path. In spite of all this, a Muslim is not sure about his eternity as it is up to Allah to decide. He guides and misleads whom he pleases (Surah 16:93). So how could I know if I was created for hell or for paradise? It was quite a dilemma. The scholars told me, "Even the prophet didn't know, so how can you, and why would you try to know?"

A SHOCKING DISCOVERY

At the age of 21, I encountered another problem. Muslims also have a lot of traditions. There are some 600,000 traditions (*Hadith*) attributed to what Muhammad did and said. Muslims follow them in obedience.

Several of the authentic reports in these traditions say that one day Muhammad said to his followers, "None of you will enter paradise through his good works."

They asked him, "What about you, O Allah's apostle?"

He replied, "Not even me, unless Allah covers me with his grace and mercy." (See the books *Sahih Bukhari* and *Sahih Muslims* in the *Hadith*).

That was a shock to me! I thought to myself, *We pray five times a day and give alms, and now I see that not one of us will enter paradise unless Allah covers us with his grace and mercy. Can I find that grace and mercy to cover me? Is there anywhere I can find this grace and mercy?* I started to check and I could not find it in the Qur'an. No Muslim could tell me how to find God's covering of grace and mercy.

> We pray five times a day and give alms, and now I see that not one of us will enter paradise unless Allah covers us with his grace and mercy.

One night I was reciting the Qur'an from memory and reached certain verses which read:

> We believe in Allah and what is revealed to us, and what was revealed to Abraham, Ismail, Isaac, and Jacob...we believe in that which was given to Moses and Jesus. We do not make any distinction (difference) among them... (Surah 3:84).

I knew these passages before, but that night my faith was questioned. I heard a voice in my mind asking me something like: "Masood, you say you believe what was revealed to Jesus and Moses, but when was the last time you acted upon it and even read what you say you believe? You on one hand claim that you do not make any distinction between the Scriptures, yet you believe that the message of Jesus and Moses is corrupted and only the message of the Qur'an is intact. Is not that making a difference or distinction? As Muslims, how can you believe in the Scriptures of Moses and Jesus if you believe that they are corrupted?"

The next day I went and got the Bible. I started reading. A flame started burning. God's Word has power. God is light, He is righteous, and what I found most of all is that God is love! He is the One who took the initiative and He first loved us. The Christian Scriptures were telling me that before I loved him, He loved me.

Muhammad said he didn't know what would happen to himself, to me, or to you. Over the next three years I continued to study the words of Jesus. I came upon where in contrast to Muhammad, Jesus says about Himself, "I know where I came from, and I know where I'm going" (see John 8:14). Muhammad, the prophet of Islam, did not give any assurance to his followers, yet Jesus said to His followers: "If you believe in Me you will have eternal life. He who follows me will not walk in darkness, but will have the light of life" (see John 6:47; 8:12). Similarly, the Bible says that God sent Jesus so *"...whoever believes in Him should not perish but have eternal life"* (John 3:16).

> Muhammad, the prophet of Islam, did not give any assurance to his followers

I also realized that a mere man was not raised to the level of divinity, but in fact Jesus, as the Word of God, and thus eternal and divine and in co-existence with God, emptied Himself and came to this world. It is because of His eternal position that Jesus had and has with God that He is divine and in co-existence with Him, thus God as the Father, Jesus as the Son, and the Holy Spirit who proceeds from the Father and the Son. *Tawhid fi al-tathlith*. Of course, just as Muslims do not have the word *Tawhid* in the Qur'an for their belief in the oneness of God, Christians do not have the word or the expression *Trinity* in their Scriptures. As Muslims chose the word *Tawhid* to explain the nature of God, so have Christians chosen *Trinity* to somewhat explain the nature of God. However, we all know that we can only go as far as our scriptures allow us. Although the Qur'an suggests that Allah is and will always be unknowable, the Christian Scriptures state that one day we will know Him as He is and that He will even abide among His people (see 1 John 3:2-3; Rev. 21:3).

One and a half billion Muslims follow a prophet who doesn't even know his own eternal destiny. And they don't know their own either. That was my dilemma. I quickly realized it is not Muhammad but Jesus who is the answer. The letter to the Hebrews says right in the beginning: "...in these last days God has spoken to us through His Son" (see Heb. 1:1-2). In fact I very soon realized that after Jesus, anyone who claims to be a prophet, if his claims and teaching do not align with the teaching of Jesus and the Scriptures, cannot be a true prophet.

> *One and a half billion Muslims follow a prophet who doesn't even know his own eternal destiny. And they don't know their own either.*

Muslims see 99 attributes of Allah, one of which is *Al-Batin* (the hidden) and the other as *Az-Zahir* (the revealed). How can God be hidden and revealed at the same time? I found the answer in the Scriptures of the Christians and of the Jews, the Bible. God revealed Himself through Jesus. It is written, *"No one has seen God at any time. The only begotten Son... He has declared Him"* (John 1:18). God the *Al-Batin* became *Az-Zahir* in Jesus. My appeal to God was what all Muslims recite in the first chapter of Qur'an: "Show me the way." In the Christian Scriptures I found that Jesus says, *"I am the way..."* (John 14:6).

GRACE AND TRUTH

Now at 21, here I was reading in the Gospel of John that the law was given through Moses and grace and truth are given through Jesus. My Islamic dilemma to find God's grace was solved. The grace and mercy that Muhammad talked about are only available through Jesus. A Savior was sent not because of the things we had done, but because of His mercy. I had not found these words anywhere else: *"Having been justified by His grace we should become heirs, according to...eternal life"* (Titus 3:7). Contrast this to Muhammad who doesn't know what will happen to him or to his people. The Qur'an told me that God leads astray whom he wishes, but the Bible says God wants all to be saved and to come to a knowledge of the truth (see 1 Tim. 2:3-4).

I found the answer for many other issues in Jesus. Above all, it was the assurance and the promise of eternal life that attracted me to follow Jesus and not Islam. At age 23, at last, I made my decision to follow Christ. I thank Him for helping me to get out of the darkness and enter into His Light.

MY FAMILY PREPARES FOR MY HONOR KILLING

Three years later, my parents asked me to come and visit them and tell them what happened. Hesitantly, I arrived home. I hadn't wanted to go; however, I sensed the Holy Spirit urging me to go the 600 miles to where my parents and 14 brothers and sisters were waiting. They asked me, "What was wrong with Islam that you left it?" Something happened. It was like someone took control of my mouth. I told them what was better with Jesus that I followed Him.

In Islam, apostates (those who leave Islam) face capital punishment. By putting my faith in Jesus, I had also harmed the honor and respect my parents had gained through the years. I remember my father gnashing his teeth and walking about the room repeating: "What will people say? A new branch in our family tree, a Christian, it is unbearable! If you were a thief, a robber, a murderer, it would not have brought the shame that you have brought upon us!" For some Muslim parents it is not just a religious duty but a matter of *izzat*—honor. Whether they are Arab or Persian, Indian or from the Far East, what people will say is the main concern.

> *A Muslim priest was there. My father asked him to perform my funeral rites.*

My father had already prepared a document to disown me for me to sign. By signing that, I lost my family name and was left with my first name, Masood, only. A Muslim priest was there. My father asked him to perform my funeral rites. I felt so empty, so detached. I knew what was happening, but I had no emotion. What was happening was that people knew an apostate had come home. A crowd was outside the house shouting, *"Murtad, qatal kar do...Allahu akbar!"* ("Apostate! Kill him! Allah is the greatest!")

MY FATHER PULLS OUT HIS SWORD TO CUT OFF MY HEAD

My father asked my brothers to blacken my face with tar and put a garland of old shoes around my neck, to portray their disgust. Then my father grabbed my collar and dragged me out in the open where people were shouting. They tied my hands and put me on a donkey there. To make an example of me, they were going to drag me with the donkey around the village. My father wanted to be admired by people as one who has given something most precious in his life. He pulled out a sword to chop off my head. At that very moment, suddenly the donkey kicked a few people, parting the crowd around me, and took off. It jumped over a broken wall and went through the next door into an outside field. Instead of going to the village, it took off with me on it into a dry stream near the river. And that's how I escaped an "honor killing" by my father. God showed me, time and again, how He knows what His people go through, and He knows how to save them in times of need.

Troubles, persecution, suffering—yes, I certainly have experienced these. Yes, my father wanted to follow the order of capital punishment for apostates in Islam. But the Lord saved me in it all.

BURIED ALIVE AND LEFT FOR DEAD

At the university campus, a few years later, not liking my testimony and conversations of how I chose to follow Jesus, some fanatical students kidnapped me, drugged me, and buried me alive! But while I was still in the grave, God rescued me by sending unexpected monsoon rains, which broke the damn on a hill above the gravesite. This caused a great deal of water to rush down and wash me up out of the grave so that I was floating in the water. Now fully alert and aware that I did not know how to swim, just then, God provided a tree branch to save me from drowning. It turned out to be a banyan tree that stood 10 feet above ground level when the water receded, but it was in the water that day to enable me to keep from drowning and climb to safety.

The next day I went back to the university campus, to where the guys were who had kidnapped, drugged, and buried me alive the day before. When these guys saw me, the look on their faces was like they saw a "dead man walking"! By then a crowd had gathered. One of them ran, one passed out, and the other was stuttering that he didn't do it and blamed the others. I raised my arm and pointed at them as the Holy Spirit prompted me to say, "You worship a god and prophet who tells you to maim and kill people, while I worship a God who saves people! My God saved me from your evil hand, but even if He didn't, I would be in eternity with Him today! What about you? Where would you be if you died? Who would save you from the same thing? No one! Think about it!" I walked out and never went back. Only God knows whose salvation benefit that was for. But one day we will know.

> *When these guys saw me, the look on their faces was like they saw a "dead man walking"! By then a crowd had gathered. One of them ran, one passed out, and the other was stuttering that he didn't do it and blamed the others.*

Because of my faith in Jesus, I often had to keep moving on to avoid persecution and also to be able to study more deeply as I met different people with whom to study. People asked me, "Are you really satisfied with this wandering life? Are you happy to live as a fugitive for the rest of your days? Is that the reason you did your research?" No, the reason for my research was only to find the truth, that truth which would set me free from the empty way of life handed down by my forefathers. God Himself opened my heart and mind to the straight path, the way He chose before the creation of the world through which humankind could be reconciled with Him—Jesus Christ, who shared in our humanity so that by His death He could destroy the power of satan and free those who have been held in slavery to his ways all their lives.

Since becoming a Christian I have become acutely aware of my un-worthiness, but at the same time I know that, in God's eyes, my value is great. That is why He tells me through His Word:

> *I tell you, do not worry about your life, what you will eat or drink; or about your body, what you will wear. Is not life more important than food, and the body more important than clothes? Look at the birds of the air; they do not sow or reap or store away in barns, and yet your heavenly Father feeds them. Are you not much more valuable than they?* (Matthew 6:25-26 NIV)

I know that this life I have is not my own. I have given it willingly to Jesus, and He knows what is best for me. Although I have lost my original family and although there have been many threats against me, my Lord comforts me. His Word says:

> *Do not be afraid of those who kill the body but cannot kill the soul. Rather, be afraid of the One who can destroy both soul and body in hell. Are not two sparrows sold for a penny? Yet not one of them will fall to the ground apart from the will of your Father. And even the very hairs of your head are all numbered. So don't be afraid; you are worth more than many sparrows* (Matthew 10:28-31 NIV).

In all of life's troubles, perplexities, and temptations, and in loneliness, weariness, and disappointments, He comes to rescue us, and I praise Him for this. Like the apostle Paul, I am able to say—even though I am beaten, yet I am not killed; though at times I am sorrowful, yet I am always rejoicing; though poor, I have been given the opportunity to make many rich by sharing the Gospel; though I have nothing, yet as a child of God I possess everything; should I die, yet will I live on. I can consider everything a loss compared to the surpassing greatness of knowing Christ Jesus my Lord. He does not want anyone to perish, but wants all to be saved and to come to knowledge of the truth (see 2 Cor. 6:9-10; Phil. 3:8; 1 Tim. 2:3-4).

Indeed it is the Bible, the Judeo-Christian Scriptures that tell how God offers all people the assurance of forgiveness of sins. Today when you hear His voice, harden not your heart (see Ps. 95:7-8; Heb. 4:7).

COMMENTARY BY FAISAL MALICK

Steven's scholarship and study over many years in search of truth is to be commended. He investigated the Qur'an, the writings of Moses, and the words of Jesus. Through careful research and analysis he became fully persuaded that Jesus is the only way to obtain the grace and mercy of God and know truth. His commitment to his decision has cost him much, but it cannot be compared with what he has gained in Christ. From escaping an honor killing to being buried alive and left for dead, he lives to share his story with us today.

> *How could Allah command us in the Qur'an to have equal faith with the previous books that came from Heaven if they are corrupted?*

Your journey to freedom begins with a divinely inspired thought. For Steven it was a series of such thoughts and questions that kept him on the path to seeking truth. One contemplative thought in particular was, *How could Allah command us in the Qur'an to have equal faith with the previous books that came from Heaven if they are corrupted?* This question made him look at the Bible with a fresh perspective, as the Bible contains the other three books that Muslims believe came from Heaven. This is when Steven began to find the answers to all his heart's questions about God and eternal life. The Bible says it this way:

> *For the law was given through Moses; grace and truth*
> *came through Jesus Christ* (John 1:17 NIV).

Before Jesus the Word of God came to earth and took on flesh, an angel visited Zacharias, the father of John the Baptist, while he was in the temple carrying out his priestly duties. As mentioned earlier, John the Baptist was a prophet who is revered in both the Qur'an and the Bible. Before his birth there had been no communication from God through any prophets for 400 years since the prophet Malachi. This was a time of divine silence from Heaven for the earth.

When the angel appeared to Zacharias in the temple, he was already too old to have children and he was married to Elizabeth who was barren (see Luke 1:7). Let's look at the whole Bible account of the story of Zacharias' encounter with Gabriel, an archangel of God.

> *Then an angel of the Lord appeared to him, standing on*
> *the right side of the altar of incense. And when Zacharias*
> *saw him, he was troubled, and fear fell upon him. But*
> *the angel said to him, "Do not be afraid, Zacharias, for*
> *your prayer is heard; and your wife Elizabeth will bear*
> *you a son, and you shall call his name John. And you*
> *will have joy and gladness, and many will rejoice at his*
> *birth. For he will be great in the sight of the Lord, and*
> *shall drink neither wine nor strong drink. He will also*
> *be filled with the Holy Spirit, even from his mother's*
> *womb. And he will turn many of the children of Israel*
> *to the Lord their God. He will also go before Him in*
> *the spirit and power of Elijah, 'to turn the hearts of*
> *the fathers to the children,' and the disobedient to the*
> *wisdom of the just, to make ready a people prepared for*
> *the Lord." And Zacharias said to the angel, "How shall*

I know this? For I am an old man, and my wife is well advanced in years." And the angel answered and said to him, "I am Gabriel, who stands in the presence of God, and was sent to speak to you and bring you these glad tidings. But behold, you will be mute and not able to speak until the day these things take place, because you did not believe my words which will be fulfilled in their own time" (Luke 1:11-20).

John the Baptist was called by God to prepare the way of the Lord Jesus, or Yeshua, which is Hebrew for Jesus and means "salvation."

Notice that the news God announces after 400 years of silence from Heaven is that Zacharias is going to have a son by the name of John. This revered prophet's name, *John*, means, "Yahweh is grace and mercy." This is very significant because when God names someone it is always connected to his or her destiny. John the Baptist was called by God to prepare the way of the Lord Jesus, or *Yeshua*, which is Hebrew for Jesus and means "salvation." So God was saying through the birth of John that He is gracious, answering the prayers of humankind and preparing the way for salvation by providing grace and truth in the person of Jesus. This is the answer Steven was looking for all his life and he finally found it in Jesus Christ.

Your prayers are waiting to be answered in the person of Jesus Christ who is returning soon. Jesus is the Alpha and the Omega, the Beginning and the End. He is the Word who became flesh to die on the Cross and arose again to the right hand of God. He is now reaching out to you with grace and love through this book.

The following verse from the *Zabur* (Psalms) of the prophet David describes Steven's journey to truth.

Your word is a lamp to my feet and a light to my path (Psalms 119:105).

Whether you take years of research or you have a sudden vision of Jesus, the most important thing is to believe in Jesus and surrender your life to Him with all your heart.

> *Father God, I thank You for each person who is reading this book and now I also ask that You bless him or her with understanding of who Jesus truly is and that each of them has his or her own story to tell of how he came to know You and what You are going to do in his life, in Jesus' name. Amen.*

THE PRIMARY PURPOSE OF THIS book is to reveal the heart and love that God has for the Muslim people. However, the full extent of this book is to testify of God's love and mercy which is available to all humankind.

> *In the past God spoke to our forefathers through the prophets at many times and in various ways, but in these last days He has spoken to us by His Son, whom He appointed heir of all things, and through whom also He made the universe. The Son is the radiance of God's glory and the exact representation of His being, sustaining all things by His powerful word. After he had provided purification for sins, He sat down at the right hand of the Majesty in heaven* (Hebrews 1:1-3 NIV).

You have heard God speak through His prophets, but are you hearing Him speak through His Son?

You have just read the stories of ten amazing Muslims touched by God. What makes our stories amazing is not our background but the sovereign way in which we came to a revelation of Jesus Christ. Granted, not everyone has such supernatural experiences in coming to know God, but out of the millions who have, these are written so you might believe!

> ... *This is the work of God, that you believe in Him whom He sent* (John 6:29).

Let me share with you a dream a prominent Muslim had that changed his life. In his dream he kept trying to climb a fence and reach the other side, but he could not and kept falling to the ground. He tried over and over again, but no matter how many times he tried he just kept falling to the ground. He sensed in his dream that it was very important for him to get to the other side of the fence. Then he suddenly awoke. He knew God was speaking to him through the dream so he went about seeking the meaning. He finally came to a church and inquired of the pastor if he could perhaps help. The pastor was able to interpret the dream.

This is what the pastor shared with him:

> "You are trying to get to Heaven through your good deeds and works but you cannot, and that is why you keep falling to the ground. The only way to Heaven is to receive the gift of salvation through the grace of Jesus Christ."

This Muslim along with five other Muslim friends surrendered their lives to Jesus and secured their eternal salvation.

Heaven is accessed through grace and not through good works. There is only one work that is acceptable to God and that is to believe in Jesus.

In the words of John, one of the closest disciples of Jesus:

> *We proclaim to you the One who existed from the beginning, whom we have heard and seen. We saw Him with our own eyes and touched Him with our own hands. He is the Word of life. This One who is life itself was revealed to us,*

and we have seen Him. And now we testify and proclaim to you that He is the One who is eternal life. He was with the Father, and then He was revealed to us. We proclaim to you what we ourselves have actually seen and heard so that you may have fellowship with us. And our fellowship is with the Father and with His Son, Jesus Christ (1 John 1:1-3 NLT).

The inspiration of this book has been for you to know the sweet fellowship that can be had with the Father and His Son Jesus Christ. Entering into a relationship with God also results in the fellowship that is shared among those whose joy knows that we all belong to Him—and to one another—forever.

> Heaven is accessed through grace and not through good works. There is only one work that is acceptable to God and that is to believe in Jesus.

If you have not already done so and you would like to know God in the way these stories have made you aware is possible, would you pray this final prayer with me?

Dear Heavenly Father, You are the Most High God, and I come to You in the name of Jesus. I thank You for sending Jesus to the earth as the Word of God who became flesh. Father, I receive Your love and gift of salvation in the person of Jesus Christ. Jesus, I believe You died on a Cross and shed Your blood for my sins and the sins of the whole world. I believe God raised You from the dead on the third day. Jesus, come into my heart. Take away my stony heart and give me a new heart that I may love the Father even as You do.

My prayer for you.

Father, I thank You in the name of Jesus that Your Spirit will witness with my brother or sister that he or she is a child of God. Father, make known to him Your ways and show him Your covenant. Manifest Your Presence and touch him deeply with Your Holy Spirit and unveil Your Word to him continually. Let him taste and see that You are good. Amen.

Welcome to the family of God!

I look forward to meeting you in Heaven one day, if not sooner.

Faisal Malick
www.amazingmuslims.com

Now to Him who is able to keep you from stumbling, and to make you stand in the presence of His glory blameless with great joy, to the only God our Savior, through Jesus Christ our Lord, be glory, majesty, dominion and authority, before all time and now and forever. Amen (Jude 1:24-25 NASB).

CONTACT INFORMATION

Cemil and Isil Akbulut

Email: Office@TurkishRevival.org
Website: http://trmin.org/trm/

Jaafar Attaran

Pastor, Iranian Christian Church of Central Florida
Office Phone: (407) 951-5025
Email: IranianChurchOrlando@cfl.rr.com

Güçlü Corey Erman

Founder, Turkish Revival Ministries
Pastor, The River at Istanbul Church, Istanbul, Turkey
Oversight of churches, Bible schools, television and media ministries.
Email: Office@TurkishRevival.org
Website: http://trmin.org/trm/

Hamdi Erman

The River at Istanbul Church, Istanbul, Turkey
Email: Office@TurkishRevival.org
Website: http://trmin.org/trm/

Faisal Malick

Website: www.faisalmalick.com

To respond to this book or for further information please visit Faisal Malick's
Website at www.amazingmuslims.com

Dr. Steven Masood

Email: sm@itl-usa.org

Website: www.JesusToMuslims.org

Author of several books including *The Bible and the Qur'an: A Question of
Integrity.* His autobiography *Into the Light* is available in several languages.

Mohammed Seyedzadeh

Email: mitiasi@yahoo.com

Kamal Saleem

Founder, Koome Ministries: Education, training, and media

Websites: www.kamalsaleem.com and www.Koomeministries.com

Author of two books: *In The Red Chair* and *Blood of the Lambs: A Former Terrorist's Memoirs of Death and Redemption*. Please see Koome's website for other materials by Kamal Saleem.

Akef Tayem

Founder, Sons of Abraham Ministries

Email: akeftayem@msn.com

Website: www.sonsofabraham.com

Author of: *From the Crescent to the Cross: A Palestinian's Journey.*

Khalida Wukawitz

Email: khalidajesuslove@yahoo.com

Website: www.truthunveiled.net